Process Modeling for Business Analysts Made Easy

Determining Business Requirements without Pain

Trond Frantzen

Cataloguing-in-Publication Data

Copyright © 2017 **Trond Frantzen**.

Process Modeling for Business Analysts Made Easy: Determining Business Requirements without Pain

1. Process Modeling
2. Business process modeling
3. Business analysis
4. Business requirements analysis
5. Business requirements elicitation
6. Business requirement process modeling
7. Business requirements analysis methodology
8. Business requirement

You can reach Trond Frantzen at the address below:

Trond.Frantzen@PowerstartGroup.com

Table of Contents

Process Modeling for Business Analysts Made Easy

Determining Business Requirements without Pain

Trond Frantzen

About the Author

Trond Frantzen is a business development strategist, a leadership consultant, and an author. He is the Managing Partner of the PowerStart Group, a company that focuses on business development and requirements analysis. He is also the author of several business books, and has delivered strategic consulting services to scores of clients; and conducted interactive courses and seminars with over 35,000 people.

Trond was born in Norway, raised in Toronto's west end, graduated from Concordia University, lives in Calgary (the heart of the New West) and is connected to a very large social network of friends and acquaintances.

As a professional with many years of business consulting experience, and a finalist in the *Entrepreneur of the Year* Oakville Awards of Business Excellence, Trond has been recognized by many professional associations.

You can connect with Trond on LinkedIn at http://www.linkedin.com/in/trondfrantzen

Or you can email him at Trond.Frantzen@PowerstartGroup.com

Also by Trond Frantzen. Available from Amazon.

Part 1.
The Business Event

Many people say business process modeling is challenging, difficult and requires a lot of practice. They have been saying this for years, and there are scores of books showing exactly how difficult and complex it can be.

But this simply isn't true.

Yes, we do have to practice. That's true for any method in any profession. But knowing how to do it is a simple, straight-forward process that can be learned by anyone who has a fundamental understanding of business.

There are really only four elements we need to know about to create accurate and effective Business Process Models: (1) The **Business Event**; (2) the **Business Object**; (3) the **Business Rules Table**; and, (4) the **Process Model** itself.

Throw away the confusion infused by so many other books, videos and courses. This book is definitely not technical – because it doesn't have to be. You will not get lost in the depths of technical jargon, nor in technical methodologies reserved for software engineers and database designers.

You can tackle this book on your own or with a group of your peers. You can do it on your own schedule, when the time suits you. You can do it at the office, or at home, or in a coffee shop, on the bus or the train – anywhere at all.

I understand that we're all wired a little different and we learn in different way. Accordingly, I've combined text and graphic in a way to make life easy.

We all live in a serial world. Because of this, we tend to do things in chronological order. This creates a challenge when it comes to analysis of any kind. Gathering information (sometimes a bit fuzzy) and synthesizing it into some kind of knowledge we can deal with is definitely not a sequential process. The fact is, when we assimilate information we are constantly jumping in and out of different "states" of knowledge. We then put the information we gather into one context or another based on the *situations*, *conditions* and *circumstances* that give the information contextual meaning. Primarily, this is because our work (in the world of analysis) consists of contextual knowledge rather than the serial assembly of things.

Our knowledge repository – our brain – is like a neural network consisting of nodes with access paths that are busy (strong) or not so busy (weak). This neural network becomes our 'organized memory' with keys to join bits and pieces of data to form cohesive information (we hope), and blocks of information from which we can extrapolate contextual knowledge.

In terms of functionality, data storage and desired results, computerized systems are not much different from the human brain. Computerized systems – as is also true for non-automated systems – must store data (i.e., *remember things*) to support various *conditions* and *circumstances* they have to deal with. In the context of business analysis, these are called ***business events***.

1.1 Where to Start

A *business event* is an essential business condition, a state, circumstance, situation or requirement that exists – which the target business unit must respond to or deal with in order to carry on operations to successfully support its key business objectives, goals, mission, direction and vision. A *business event* transcends time and technology; i.e., it does not reflect **_how_** something is done; it represents **_what_** must be done without regard to a particular technology.

To summarize, a *business event* is:

1) a state, condition, circumstance, situation or requirement that exists;
2) essential (critical) to the business; and
3) based on time, a decision, situation or third party need.

To you as a business analyst, recognizing a *business event* is fundamental to the work you have to do. So, let's explore the different kinds of *business events* and, ultimately, what we do with them.

1.2 The Business Events

Business events come in four flavors:

1) **Situation Business Event** – non-controlled
   "The Customer Buys a Product"
   "The Customer Has Exceeded Their Credit Limit"

2) **External Business Event** – based on 3rd party need
   "The Customer Requests a Higher Credit Limit"

3) **Temporal Business Event** – based on time
   "The Customer's Credit Card Expires"
   "It is Time to Increase the Customer's Credit
   Limit"

4) **Internal Business Event** – based on a decision
   "The Company Decides to Cancel the Customer's
   Credit Card"

Note in the examples above that a *business event* **never**
starts with a verb. That's because a *business event* is not
a process. Let's be clear. A *business event* is a condition,
state, situation or circumstance that must be supported
by a process. (A process, which we'll discuss later, does
start with a verb and can support one or more *business
events*.)

When a *business event* is identified we don't need to
label it as one of the four kinds of *business events* listed
above. We leave it unlabeled because, to a client or
anyone else who is reading the documentation, a
business event is simply a *business event*. It's a business
circumstance. We don't need to tell them it's temporal
or external or anything else. They don't care.

So, why do we have labels (*situation, external,
temporal, internal*) for the four different kinds of
business events then?

Because it gives you, the business analyst, an
opportunity to process what kind of situation or
circumstance – *business event* – we are really dealing
with.

For example, what's the difference between "**The
Company Decides to Pay a Supplier**" and "**It is Time
to Pay a Supplier**"? These are two different *business*

events that sound the same, but are actually very different.

The first one (an internal *business event* based on a decision) suggests that there is a decision point, and this decision must be reflected in the subsequent process model. The second one (an internal *business event* based on time) suggests that there is no decision involved, it's just <u>time</u> to pay the supplier – perhaps the goods ordered have been received, and it is therefore time to pay the supplier. Whatever the time criteria, this too must be reflected somehow in the supporting process model.

By assessing the type of *business event*, we are able to think through the ramifications and reflect this in the resulting business process model.

The most common type of *business event* used by those who are new to this kind of analysis is the temporal *business event* that starts with "**It is Time to …**".

While this truly is a very common type of *business event*, it is also the most common error, mostly because it is simply so easy – and a lazy way – to identify a *business event* as "**It is Time to … (something)**". For example, I have often seen *business events* such as "**It is Time to Receive a Product Shipment from a Supplier**" when it clearly should be "**Product Shipment Arrives from a Supplier**". The arrival of the shipment from the supplier, while expected, is somewhat out of our control, therefore it is an external *business event*. To state "**It is Time to Receive a Product Shipment from a Supplier**" seems a bit awkward and certainly doesn't have the same meaning as "**Product Shipment Arrives from a Supplier**". On the other hand, a *business event* such as, "**It is Time for a Product Shipment from a Supplier to Arrive**" is something else again. This kind of *business event* <u>is</u> within our control, and we must have a planned response for it.

Carefully thinking through the type of *business event* we're dealing with is therefore helpful in stating it well.

1.3 Use Cases and You

Business events that are identified to be part of a project's scope are supported by processes and data. In other words, the *business event* is the identified <u>circumstance</u> or <u>condition</u> that the system has to deal with. How the business system "deals with" a *business event* is described, partially, by a diagram that illustrates the supporting business process and data.

It's interesting to note that different notational standards have developed to illustrate a system's processes and data.

The most commonly used and most popular diagramming convention is *Use Case* notation, which was originally intended to specify software systems, not business systems.

More recently, *Business Use Cases* have been introduced. However, from a business perspective – in my opinion – this hasn't been too successful (although many software engineers claim they like it a whole lot) since most IT professionals are using *Use Cases* to specify business requirements with a lot of "how" (the solution architecture) built in. While *Use Cases* theoretically see the target system as a "black box" (i.e., no implementation details or "how" things are done), the fact is this is rarely the case.

The other issue, in my opinion, is that the use of *Use Cases* simply takes too long and the documentation is not very business-friendly. *Use Cases* and most other analysis methodologies have been developed to assist with software development, not for business development or improvement.

In any event, *Use Case* usage is well documented, with hundreds of books available. The fact remains that *Use Cases* are derived from the foundations that came from data modeling and process modeling. That being the case, the subsequent discussion will illustrate a unique approach to business analysis and process modeling which will enable us to be clearly non-physical in our approach to our work.

1.4 A Basic Business Event

Before we go on to the details of how to determine full-scale business requirements, let's look at a small, isolated example that's based on a single *business event*.

The *business event*: **A Customer Buys a Product**

The customer enters a shoe store, finds the right shoes (for example, lime green loafers, size 13), and buys them. The customer pays for the shoes. The sales person asks the customer for their phone number and name, and determines if they are already in the store's system. If they are not in the system, the sales person asks the customer for information (such as name, address, phone number, etc.) and enters it in the system. When the customer buys the shoes, and the payment is recorded, the store inventory for 'Lime Green Loafers, Size 13' is reduced by the quantity bought by the customer.

We also need to track the outlet where the customer bought the shoes (so we can have store sales statistics); and we need to know which sales person served the customer (so we can figure out commissions).

That's the scenario. Now, how does the process model for this look?

Process diagrams must show the data that's needed to support a specific circumstance (*business event*), as well as where the data comes from and what you do with it. Accordingly, we have to ask the following question to get us started with the diagram:

> 1. How do I know that a "**A Customer Buys a Product**"?

This is followed by two follow-on questions:

> 2. What do I want to do about it?
> 3. What do I need to remember or record?

After these initial questions, we start by just drawing an unlabelled circle (a bubble) to represent the process that's going to support the *business event* "**A Customer Buys a Product**".

Fig. 1: Business Process Diagram – Sell Product

The answer to the initial question, *"How do I know that ... **a Customer buys a product**?"* is that a customer shows up in the store and asks for the lime green loafers, size 13. We can draw this as shown in Fig. 2.

(Just follow along for now. We're going to discuss the details of this process later in the book.)

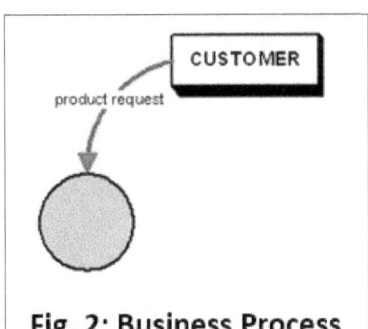

Fig. 2: Business Process Diagram – Sell Product

The next question, *"What do I want to do about it?"* requires that you think through all the things you need to do: Check if the customer is already in our database; find the lime green loafers in inventory (size 13) and give them to the customer; get a payment for the purchase; record the store in which the transaction took place, and remember which sales person served the customer.

From a technology perspective, it doesn't matter at this time if this happens in a brick-and-mortar store or online.

Let's start by determining if the customer is already on file with us, with the following diagram:

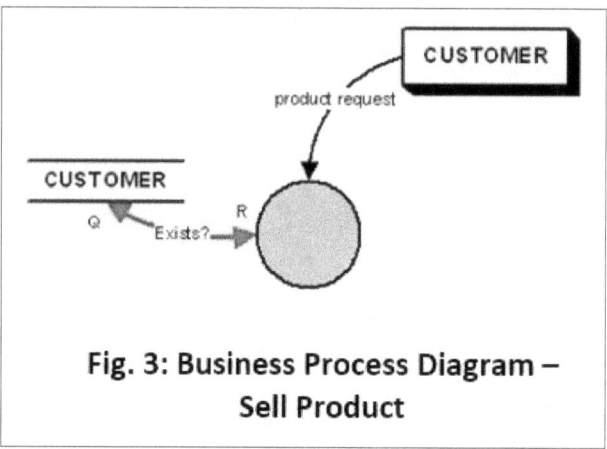

Fig. 3: Business Process Diagram – Sell Product

If they are not already recorded, get the customer's information and record it.

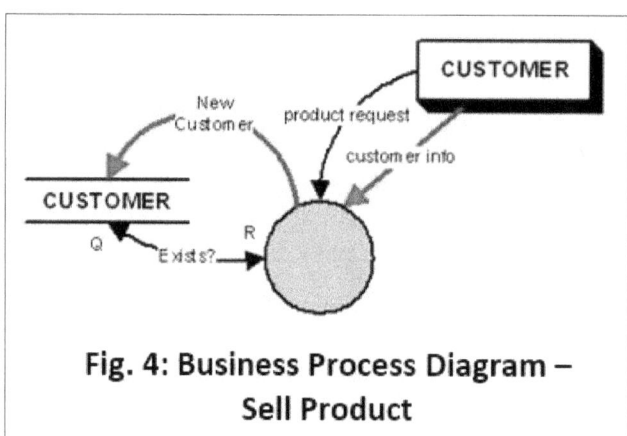

Fig. 4: Business Process Diagram – Sell Product

Get the lime green loafers from inventory, and give the
shoes and the price to the customer.

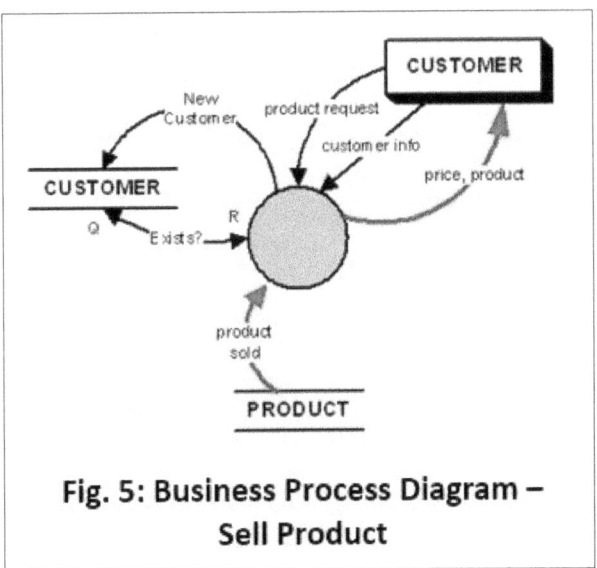

**Fig. 5: Business Process Diagram –
Sell Product**

Decrease the shoe inventory.

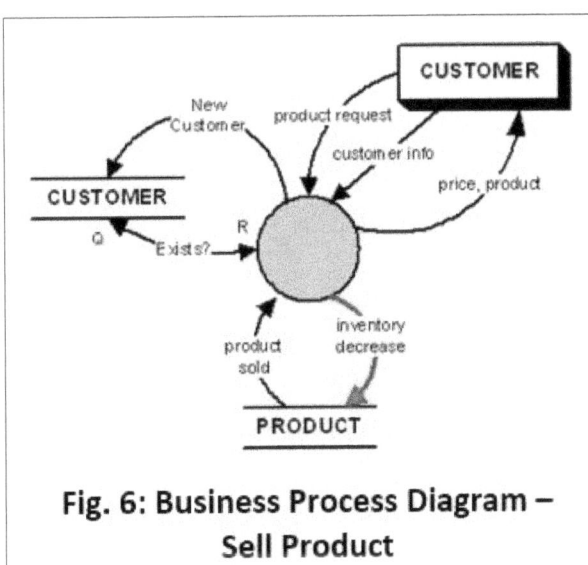

**Fig. 6: Business Process Diagram –
Sell Product**

Receive the payment from the customer, and record it.

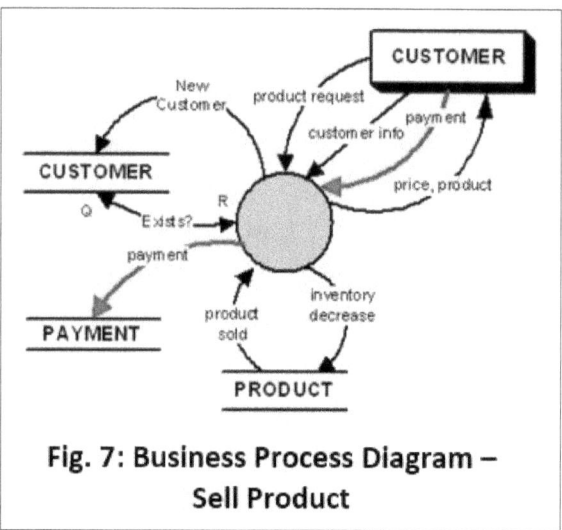

**Fig. 7: Business Process Diagram –
Sell Product**

Connect the store where the transaction took place, and the salesperson who served the customer.

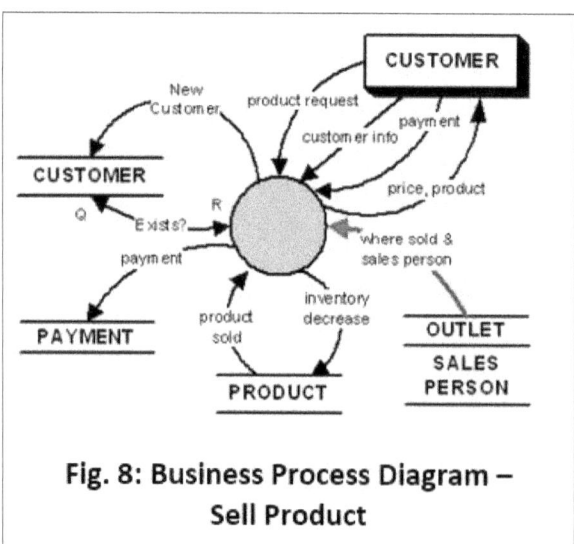

**Fig. 8: Business Process Diagram –
Sell Product**

There's the whole diagram. Now we just need to label it, inside the bubble, with a strong and pointy name to define what this process actually does. Again, I'm going to just label it ***sell product***.

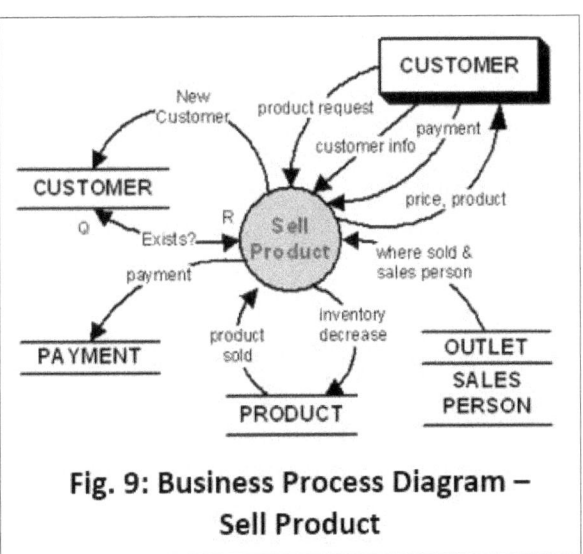

**Fig. 9: Business Process Diagram –
Sell Product**

A picture might be worth a thousand words, but we can't leave the understanding of this diagram to chance or someone's intuition, so we still have to write the narrative for the process – which could read as follows:

For each request for a product from the customer:
- Find out if the **customer** exists in our system
- Find the **product** sold
- If it is available, give the **product** to the **customer** with the price
- Accept the **payment** from the **customer**
- Remember the **payment**
- Remember the **salesperson** who served the **customer**, and in which **outlet**
- Reduce inventory by the quantity of **product** sold
- If it is a new **customer**, get the customer information from the **customer**.
- Remember the new **customer** information.

There's a specific way of determining the narrative, which we'll discuss in detail later. It certainly isn't some kind of stream of consciousness text. How we determine the process narrative is very precise.

As you are going through this process of drawing the diagram and writing the narrative, you also progressively identify the Objects (**CUSTOMER, PAYMENT, PRODUCT, OUTLET,** and **SALESPERSON**), defining and attributing data to them, such as **CUSTOMER** in Fig. 10.

CUSTOMER
Someone who requests or buys product or service from the company

<u>Business Rules</u>

- may be served by one or more **salespersons**
- may never be served by a **salesperson** (e g , the customer never buys anything)
- must have been in one or more **outlets**
- may buy one or more **products**
- may never buy a **product** (but must have requested something that was unavailable)
- may make several **payments** for **products** purchased
- may never make a **payment** for a **product** (e.g., didn't buy anything; or returned a defective product)

<u>Data Attributes</u>

- customer name
- customer address
- phone number

Fig. 10: Object Description – Customer

Once this is done you build the **Business Rules Table** by allocating the business rules to the individual Objects.

BRT		Salesperson	Customer	Outlet	Product	Payment
1	Salesperson		N	1,N	N	N
1	Customer	1,N,0		1,N	1,N,0	1,N,0
1	Outlet	N	N		N	N
1	Product	1,N,0	1,N,0	1,N		1,N,0
1	Payment	1,N	1	1	1,N	

Fig. 11: Business Rules Table – "Sell Product" Business Process

I'll explain everything about the **Business Rules Table** later, in Part 3.

In my opinion, **Business Process Diagrams** are very useful and business-friendly when describing a business process.

Part 2.
The Business Object

The first step in business system analysis is not to find out **how** the system will function – the first step is to find *what we need to **know*** in order to support the conditions or circumstances that the business will encounter. In other words, we can't just say, *"what do you want the system to do?"* We first have to determine the circumstances and conditions the business has to support, and then we'll figure out how it's going to support those circumstances and conditions.

Figuring out <u>what</u> the business must support is called "analysis". Arriving at a solution as to <u>how</u> the system will do it is called "design" or "architecture". Determining what is needed must always come <u>before</u> determining how to accomplish it – *"form follows function,"* as the great architect Louis H. Sullivan wrote.

System design is by definition a solution; and a system solution (*how* the system does what it's supposed to do) is very physical. Business analysis, on the other hand, is obtaining knowledge and therefore not at all physical … at least, not yet. Analysis uncovers **what we need to know** about a planned approach to a business situation or circumstance, in all its composite pieces; but it is not about how the system will behave. Our analysis, therefore, must be completely free of any implementation bias, or we start trying to mix apples with sheep. What I mean by this is that clarity of thought (without an implementation bias) will always help us get the <u>business requirements</u> done faster and better.

And "faster and better" should be the foundation for any approach to business requirements analysis. The best way I know of maintaining clear and focused thought is to not mix the complexities of a potential design solution with the essential business requirements. How to do this will become clear as we progress.

2.1 How to Use a Business Event

We have traditionally called the result of analysis the *system* or *business specification* – because, we presume, it should be specific. The problem, however, is that it has too often been a *generalization* – and much too focused on the *system* aspect of the business; i.e., a statement of the physical environment with general system behavior added. Well, that's been a problem.

To discover the real and complete needs of an organizational unit or a business initiative, all questions and the resulting specification must be put in a specific business context to be understandable. This context will be in what we call a *business event*.

A *business event* is an essential <u>condition</u>, a <u>circumstance</u>, a <u>state</u>, a <u>situation</u> or an <u>external requirement</u> that exists which the business must respond to or deal with in order to carry on operations to successfully meet its key business objectives, goals, mission, direction and vision. A *business event* does not consider or reflect technology or specific time; i.e., it does not reflect **how** something is done; it exclusively focuses on **what** must be done without regard to a particular technology or implementation.

In summary, a *business event* is:

1) a state, circumstance, condition, situation or external requirement that exists;
2) essential (critical) to the business; and
3) based on when something happens, a decision, a situation or a third-party need.

All *business events* have a specific structure. To reflect this structure, they come in four different flavors. These are:

Situation Business Event (non-controlled)

- "The Customer Buys a Product"
- "The Customer Has Exceeded Their Credit Limit"

External Business Event (based on third party need)

- "The Customer Requests a Higher Credit Limit"

Temporal Business Event (based on when something happens)

- "The Customer's Credit Card Expires"
- "It is Time to Increase the Customer's Credit Limit"

Internal Business Event (based on a decision)

- "The Company Decides to Cancel the Customer's Credit Card"

Our first analysis objective on a project is to find just a few *business events* to start with. Although finding as many *business events* as possible is desirable, we don't need to find more than a handful. Once a few have been found, all others will follow. We'll discuss this concept in more detail when we look at **The Business Rules Table** in Part 3.

Some other examples of *business events* are:

- A Customer *buys* a Product
- It is Time to *order* a Product from a Supplier
- The Product *arrives* from the Supplier
- An Employment Application *arrives*
- The Company *closes* the Customer's Account

Business event statements consist of nouns and verbs. The nouns usually become Objects (which we'll discuss later), while the verb indicates the context of the process that supports the *business event*.

Note in the examples above that a *business event* never starts with a verb. That's because a *business event* is not a process. It doesn't do anything. A *business event* is a circumstance, condition, state or external requirement that must be supported by a process. But before we try specifying a business process, we need to know what business condition or situation we want to support with that process.

Why are there 4 different flavors of *business events*?

When a *business event* is identified we don't need to label it as this or that kind of *business event* – whether it is Situation, External, Temporal or Internal. Why not? Because, to the organization you are working with and your clients, a *business event* is simply a *business event*. It doesn't need labeling. So why do we have names for the four different kinds of *business events* then? Because it gives you, the analyst, an opportunity to process and think through what kind of *business event* we are really dealing with; and it allows me (in writing this book) to refer to each of the four different kinds of *business events* by a distinct name. But our clients (the business folks and stakeholders) don't care, so it's unnecessary to label them in any documentation that you produce.

But there are distinct differences between the different kinds of *business events* – and that's why I've given them different labels; therefore, it's important to phrase the *business event* correctly.

For example, there's a clear difference between "**The Company Decides to Pay the Supplier**" and "**It is Time to Pay the Supplier**". The first one (an Internal *business event*) suggests that there is a decision point, and this decision point must be reflected in the business specification. The second one (a Temporal *business event*) suggests that there is no decision point, it's just <u>time</u> to pay the supplier – perhaps the time criteria is 30 days after receiving goods from the supplier; or it's "time" to do so immediately after receipt of goods from the supplier. Whatever the time criteria, this too must eventually be reflected in the business specification. By identifying the type of *business event* you are working with, you are then able to more clearly think through the ramifications on the specification.

Start with a short list of potential *business events* for the project

For most projects, it's usually helpful to start with a list of *business events* longer than just a couple. This will give a project a kick-start to get it off the ground. To arrive at a potential list of *business events* you need to do some brainstorming, applying a lot of imagination. Your general knowledge about the subject area or target business area will be a great help. One way of brainstorming a project's potential *business events* is to look at your history of *business events* from previous projects. (Yes, you should keep a **Master Business**

Events List for your organization.) If you have a Master Business Events List, review each of the *business events* on that list and see how many of them might fit your project. For each *business event* on your master list, change the nouns to fit your project. If you think you have a *business event* that's within the scope of your project include it on your list of potential *business events*.

If you don't yet have a Master Business Events List, send me an email and I'll send you one with about 4,000 business events from different industries (businesses we've worked with) and subject areas. You can reach me at trond.frantzen@powerstartgroup.com. I'm happy to help.

Don't worry about finding all the *business events* for your project, or even if they are the right ones. Just add the ones you find to your list of potential *business events* for review with your clients and subject-matter experts in an interactive discovery session – they will tell you if a *business event* is within the scope of their planned work or not. Then eliminate those *business events* on your list that your clients or subject-matter experts have determined to be outside the scope of the project and keep the others. Remember that your list of potential *business events* can be quite long or very short in the beginning – but just a few *business events* is enough to start.

After a list of potential *business events* has been created, pick one *business event* to start with and, for that *business event*, ask your clients or subject-matter experts the following question:

"What do we need to <u>know about</u> or <u>remember</u> in order to support this business condition or circumstance?"

When you ask, *"What do we need to **know about**?"* you are looking for input information. When you ask, *"What do we need to **remember**?"* you are looking for what to record or keep track of. This question implies that you are <u>not</u> looking for the process. Your objective is to discover <u>what</u> (data) is needed to support the *business event*, not what things are to be <u>done</u> (the process).

When you ask these questions, your project subject-matter experts will respond with information that could be at the highest level of abstraction or at the lowest level of detail (right at the desktop level). It is your challenge to decipher what they have said and to determine what an Object is and what's a data attribute. More on how to do that later.

2.2 Every Process Needs Data

For each *business event* identified as part of the project's scope, we need to identify and illustrate all the data that's required to support the *business event*.

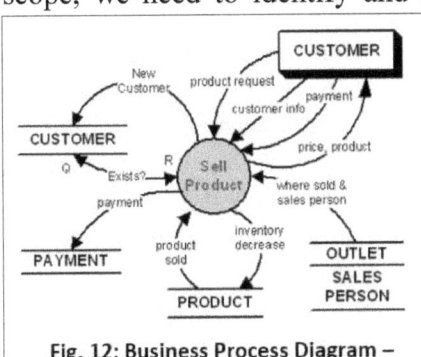

Fig. 12: Business Process Diagram – Customer Buys a Product

The relationship between Objects can be illustrated as part of a **Business Process Diagram**, like Fig. 12 (bubble in the middle, surrounded by Objects between parallel lines). More on this in Part 4, The Business Process.

What is an Object?

An Object or *entity* is a noun (i.e., a person, place, thing or concept). It is something that is *essential* or absolutely necessary in order to support the business process that in turn supports the business condition or circumstance (*business event*) found to be in-scope of your project.

An Object contains essential data and information about the business, including rules that govern the behavior of the business under specific circumstances (i.e., *business events*). Each Object is a distinct and unique collection of related data about something specific.

CUSTOMER
Someone who requests or buys product or service from the company.

Business Rules
- must be served by one or more **salespersons**
- may never be served by **salesperson** (e.g., the customer never buys anything)
- must have been in one or more **outlets**
- may buy one or more **products**
- may never buy a **product** (but must have requested something that was unavailable)
- may make several **payments** for **products** purchased
- may never make a **payment** for a **product** (e.g., didn't buy anything, or returned a defective product)

Data Attributes
- customer name
- customer address
- phone number

Unique Identifier
- customer-ID

An Object must have lots of information to describe it. It must have a <u>description</u>, so

Fig. 13: Object Description – Customer

everyone can understand what the Object is (and isn't). It must have <u>substance</u> – that is, it must consist of at least two data attributes. Each Object must also include <u>all the rules</u> that govern the business under specific circumstances (i.e., when the Object participates in various business processes with other Objects).

How to Find Objects by asking the Tracking Question

Now that we know what an Object is and what it's composed of, we can go on to the next step in gathering information from a client (or subject-matter expert), as well as how to define the Object and how to draw a picture to illustrate that each Object participates in a 'relationship' with other Objects to support a *business event*.

After a list of potential *business events* is created for the target business system, select just one *business event* (and only ever do one at a time) for which you will develop a requirements specification. For example, you may want to start with the *business event* "**A Customer Buys a Product**". Start by asking a project client or subject matter-expert (SME) the question *"What do we need to **know about** or **remember** in order to support this business circumstance?"* This is the Tracking Question. It must be specific to a *business event*. While your clients will be able to answer the question, perhaps with a little bit of prompting, be aware that they won't rush into answering this question until they are completely comfortable with what you are doing – which takes about a day of interactive 'discovery' sessions.

Also, remember that most systems only do one thing: They keep track of stuff. To keep track of stuff, the system has to record data. One of the main objectives of any business process is to remember what has been done. Remembering what has been done means recording data; and data recorded is data which is kept track of. This, in turn, enables a system to find the things we need to know.

Look and listen for nouns

The way to help your clients or SMEs move along quickly is to look for Objects in obvious places – the low-hanging fruit. The best place to start is in the *business event* statement itself. Every *business event* consists of at least a verb and a noun or two. The nouns in the *business event* statement are usually Objects, as long as they consist of two or more data items. Let's look at some examples.

"A Customer Buys a Product".

The noun **CUSTOMER** is an Object – if we can find more than one data item that belongs to it. Well, that doesn't seem too difficult – *name*, *address*, and *phone number*. That's three items (which have to be verified with a SME), so it qualifies as an Object.

CUSTOMER
Data Attributes
• customer name
• customer address
• phone number

The noun **PRODUCT** is also an Object, if we can attribute more than one data item to it. Once again, pretty easy – *product description*, *size*, and *color*. Again, with more than one data item, it qualifies as an Object.

PRODUCT
Data Attributes
• product description
• size
• color

"The Company Decides to Acquire an Asset".

The noun ASSET is an Object, if we can attribute more than one data item to it.

ASSET
Data Attributes
• asset description
• asset value
• date acquired

"The Client Opens an Account".

The nouns CLIENT and ACCOUNT are both Objects, since we can attribute more than one data item to each.

CLIENT
Data Attributes
• client legal name
• client operating name
• client address

ACCOUNT
Data Attributes
• account type
• account number
• minimum amount

"The Company Decides to Issue a Debit Card to a Customer".

The nouns CUSTOMER and DEBIT CARD are both Objects, since we can attribute more than one data item to each to describe them.

CUSTOMER
Data Attributes
• customer name
• customer address
• phone number

While DEBIT CARD is used here as an example, it is just a little bit physical – it represents the design solution to an Object which would be more correctly known as either PRODUCT or ACCOUNT – but, with the intent of communicating

DEBIT CARD
Data Attributes
• transaction amount
• transaction date
• secret PIN number

effectively with the client, I would consider it to be sufficiently useful to be included as a business Object.

What we name something conjures up specific images, and a specific image can turn into a perception (bias) of "a certain way of doing things", or an implementation bias. The word "fax" is a good example. Most of us get a certain image of a fax when we hear the word, usually involving a piece of paper that curls and falls behind the desk; whereas, the unbiased view of the technology would simply be an image or reproduction of the item. For the sake of clear analysis, it's best to stay away from words that create a specific technological image. And, seriously, who uses a fax today anyway? By tying your analysis to a specific technology, you also fix yourself in a specific point in time or history. Technology changes fast. Fundamental business requirements don't.

"It is Time to Deposit the Customer Payment to a Bank Account".

The nouns **CUSTOMER**, **PAYMENT** and **BANK ACCOUNT** are all Objects, since we can attribute more than one data item to each of them.

CUSTOMER
<u>Data Attributes</u>
• customer name
• customer address
• phone number

By helping the client discover Objects in this way you will find that they will soon get the hang of it and start contributing their own.

PAYMENT
<u>Data Attributes</u>
• payment amount
• payment date
• method of payment

BANK ACCOUNT
<u>Data Attributes</u>
• transaction amount
• transaction date
• transaction type (DR or CR)

For the *business event* "**A Customer Buys a Product**" you will find that you need information about the **PRODUCT** we sold, who we sold it to (the **CUSTOMER**), where we sold it (the **OUTLET**), who served the customer (the **SALESPERSON**), and the **PAYMENT** the customer gave us. Later, in Part 4 (The Business Process), we'll devote the whole section to discussing how to construct a **Business Process Diagram**, like the one below.

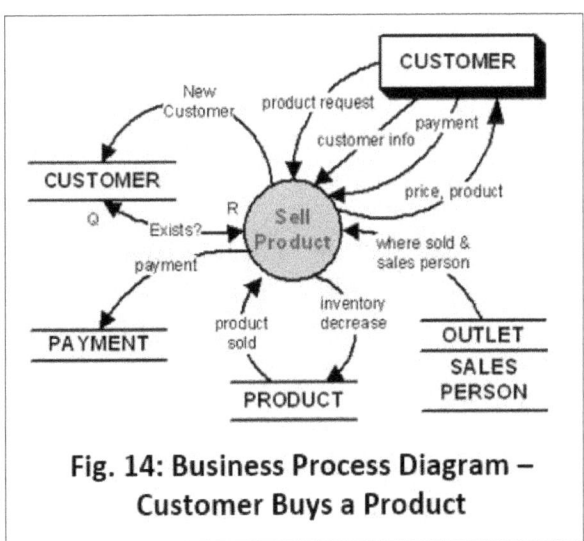

**Fig. 14: Business Process Diagram –
Customer Buys a Product**

Listen for nouns with "substance".

In any business model, every Object must have two or more data items to have "substance". Anything less than this makes it just another data attribute. So, when your client is answering your question – *"What do we need to know about or remember in order to support the business event 'A Customer Buys a Product'?"* – listen very carefully for nouns "with substance". How do you find nouns "with substance"? Ask yourself (silently, with your inside voice) whether the noun you heard can be decomposed into more than one data element. For example, when we hear the noun **CUSTOMER** can we imagine that we need several data items to describe it? Would we need to know the customer's name, address, phone number, or more? If so – and there are two or more such attributes and characteristics – then we have an Object. If not, then we just have a data item that belongs to some other Object.

It follows that not all nouns are Objects. Some are just data items that belong to and describe Objects. To determine the difference, you must ask yourself if the identified noun can be further decomposed – if you can break it down even more. If you can, it's an Object.

Objects are things that we need to <u>know about</u> or <u>remember</u>. To **know about** means we get information from an Object (as some kind of input); and we **remember** things (for future knowledge) by recording items about an Object.

Identify data attributes by listening for nouns that are not Objects.

When a client or SME answers our basic question, *"What do we need to know about or remember in order to support the <u>business event</u> 'A Customer Buys a Product'?"* – and we expand the discussion with them – they will probably tell us all about the many data items that are not Objects. For example, a client may tell us they need to know the *<u>customer name</u>* – you know immediately that this is an item that belongs to the Object **CUSTOMER**, so we attribute it to that Object.

But sometimes we just don't know where a data item belongs. When a client tells us about a series of nouns that are data items and not Objects, but are also clearly related – such as *customer name*, *address*, *phone number* – then we must "roll up" a group of related data items to form a new Object.

It's quite common to find a data item first, before identifying the Object to which it belongs. This means keeping track of stray data items, and when two or more of them seem to belong to an Object that has not yet been identified, that's the time to create and name the new Object and attribute these data items to it.

???
Data Attributes
• customer name
• customer address
• phone number

CUSTOMER
Data Attributes
• customer name
• customer address
• phone number

Ask the Inclusion Question (for Objects).

Often when discussing with a subject-matter expert the process that supports a *business event*, different Objects are mentioned, but it becomes difficult to determine if we really need to include certain Objects to support a specific business process. How can we tell? One way to determine if an Object should be included is to ask the following question:

"If we know about {the OBJECT} what will it enable us to do that we could not do if we didn't know about it?"

Let's look at an example using the *business event* "**It is Time to Deposit the Customer Payment to a Bank Account**".

First of all, are there any nouns "with substance" in the preceding *business event* statement? Reasonable candidates include the nouns **CUSTOMER**, **PAYMENT** and **BANK ACCOUNT**, since we can imagine more than one data item for each of them.

Our subject-matter expert (SME) for this example tells us that we need to keep track of the **PAYMENT**s that are **DEPOSIT**ed. We also need to know into which **BANK ACCOUNT** the payments are deposited.

As we listen to our SME we are able to identify each of these as proper Objects (they all are nouns, with substance), which we recognized to consist of two or more data attributes, or *things we want to know* about the Objects. But we aren't sure about the Object **DEPOSIT**. The word 'deposit' sounds like a verb, but if we want to *remember* the deposit then it certainly becomes a noun. So, is this really an Object, or is it what we do with the payments? How can we tell? Do we want to remember the payments deposited to the bank account? If so, does the Object **DEPOSIT** have two or more data attributes that don't appear elsewhere? What might these be? What about *date of deposit* and *name of depositor*? Do we want to remember these two items? (Our SME says yes.) Remember that a collection of two or more related data items makes a unique Object.

CUSTOMER
Data Attributes
• customer name
• customer address
• phone number

PAYMENT
Data Attributes
• payment amount
• payment date
• method of payment

BANK ACCOUNT
Data Attributes
• transaction amount
• transaction date
• transaction type (DR or CR)

DEPOSIT
Data Attributes
• date of deposit
• name of depositor
• ~~amount of deposit~~

We also want to remember (record) the *amount of deposit*, but we can determine this by taking the total of the **PAYMENT**s deposited (*payment amount*), so it would be redundant as part of **DEPOSIT**. We can't have redundancy.

What else do we need to know about the **DEPOSIT**? Although it now has two elements of data that we want to remember about it, might there be something else we want to know about it? Clearly, we need to know the **PAYMENT**s that make up the **DEPOSIT** and the **BANK ACCOUNT** the payments are deposited into. We need to remember all of this.

To verify the real need for an Object (such as **DEPOSIT**) we ask the question **"If we know about the DEPOSIT, what will it *enable* us to do that we could not do if we didn't know about it?"** In this example it clearly enables us to know about all the things we stated above – i.e., who deposited what, where and when. By asking our subject-matter expert the *Inclusion Question (for Objects)* it enables us to determine if an Object and its data are really needed to support a process.

Here is a Business Process Diagram (Fig. 15) to illustrate the data that's needed to support the "deposit" process.

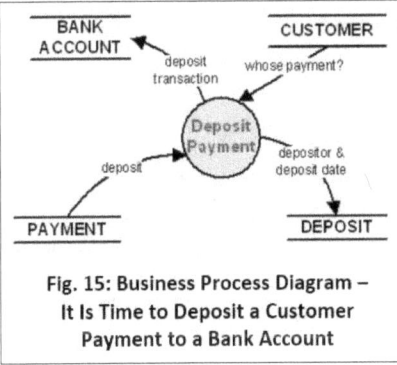

Fig. 15: Business Process Diagram –
It Is Time to Deposit a Customer
Payment to a Bank Account

Ask the <u>Exclusion</u> Question (for Objects).

This is the other side of the mirror of the *Inclusion Question (for Objects)*. It's another way of determining if an Object and its data are needed to support a process.

The *Exclusion Question (for Objects)* determines the consequences of <u>not</u> having available a specific Object, and its data, to support a business process. How can we determine the downside of <u>not</u> having available the information represented by an Object? One way to determine if an Object and its data are needed is to ask the following question:

"If we <u>do not know</u> about {the OBJECT} what will it *prevent* us from doing that we must be able to do?"

Let's look at the same example as before, **"It is Time to Deposit the Customer Payment to a Bank Account"**.

As we discussed in the previous example, we know we need to keep track of **PAYMENT**s that are deposited. We also need to know to which **BANK ACCOUNT** they are deposited. We recognize each of these nouns as Objects since they all have two or more data attributes. Just like in our previous example, however, we aren't sure about **DEPOSIT**, even though it does have the legitimate structure of an Object (i.e., it has at least two data attributes).

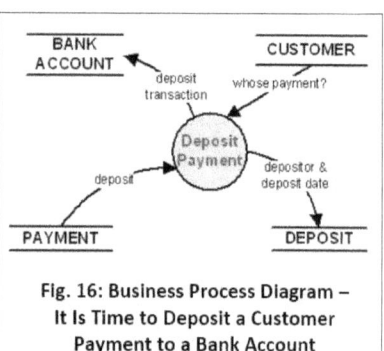

Fig. 16: Business Process Diagram – It Is Time to Deposit a Customer Payment to a Bank Account

Also, the **DEPOSIT** Object is "joined" by *foreign keys* to one or more instances of the

PAYMENT Object – so we can know which specific **PAYMENT**s make up the deposit; and to a single instance of the **BANK ACCOUNT** Object – so we can know where the **PAYMENT** was deposited; and to the **CUSTOMER** Object – so we can know to which customer the deposited payment belongs. But, still, do we really need it, the **DEPOSIT** Object? How can we be sure? To find out let's use the *Exclusion Question (for Objects)*.

"If we <u>do not know</u> about the <u>DEPOSIT</u>, what will it *prevent* us from doing that we must be able to do?"

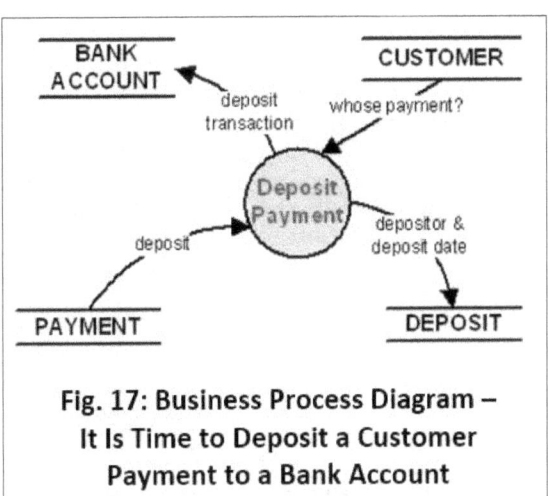

**Fig. 17: Business Process Diagram –
It Is Time to Deposit a Customer
Payment to a Bank Account**

If the **DEPOSIT** Object didn't exist – if the information wasn't available – we wouldn't know about the *date of deposit* and the *name of depositor*.

Do we need this? I suspect we do.

Without the **DEPOSIT** Object we would still be able to know that certain **PAYMENT**s are associated with specific **BANK ACCOUNT**s and **CUSTOMER**s, but we wouldn't know *by whom* the payments were deposited. Is this key information?

If your subject-matter expert says they need to know this, then the Object **DEPOSIT** must be part of the process or data relationship. Therefore, we can't exclude the Object **DEPOSIT** from participating in process that supports the *business event* "**It is Time to Deposit the Customer Payment to a Bank Account**".

On the right are examples of the Objects (with data only) that are needed to support the process "Deposit Payment" (shown in the **Business Process Diagram**, Fig. 17).

CUSTOMER

Data Attributes

- customer name
- customer address
- phone number

PAYMENT

Data Attributes

- payment amount
- payment date
- method of payment

BANK ACCOUNT

Data Attributes

- transaction amount
- transaction date
- transaction type (DR or CR)

DEPOSIT

Data Attributes

- date of deposit
- name of depositor
- ~~amount of deposit~~

The Symbiotic Relationship between Objects and Processes.

A "process" is inseparable from a "data relationship" – they have a genuine symbiotic relationship. In other words, each *business event* (i.e., circumstance or condition) that needs to be supported by the target business area must be <u>dealt with by that target business area in some manner</u> (a specific process). This always requires <u>the use of data</u> (Objects) – either to retrieve some data or to record some data. It's impossible to have a process that doesn't involve retrieving, viewing or recording of data. It's equally redundant to have data that isn't ever involved in some kind of process – something has to happen to it, otherwise why do we bother recording it?

When we include an Object in a diagram that supports a *business event,* it represents <u>all the instances</u> of that Object – its history. What distinguishes one occurrence of an Object from another may simply be a *<u>date</u>*.

In the **Business Process Diagram** in Fig. 18, for example, the Object **PAYMENT** can be seen as one or more instances of **PAYMENT**s; we can therefore see it as a <u>list</u> of all the payments (i.e., all its occurrences). Equally, the **CUSTOMER** and **PRODUCT** Objects can be seen as <u>lists</u> of all the customers

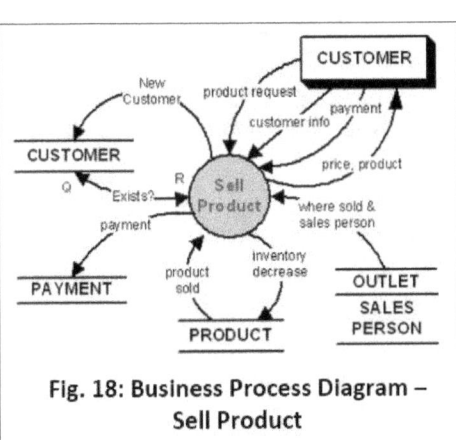

Fig. 18: Business Process Diagram – Sell Product

that we have done business with and all the products that we have sold to those customers.

Objects are always named and documented in the singular since we always view them as *one or more instances* of an Object and, as we will learn later when we discuss the **Business Rules Table** in Part 3, we always ask questions about an Object as if there was only a single instance of that Object.

Summary of How to Find Business Events and Objects

1. **Create a short list of potential *business events* for the project.** Don't worry about finding all the *business events* that are in-scope – just start with a few. You only need a few *business events* to find all the others, as you will see when we discuss the **Business Rules Table** in Part 3.

   After an initial list of potential *business events* has been created, pick one *business event* to start with and ask the project subject-matter experts (the ones who have knowledge in the context of the chosen *business event*) the following question:

   "What do we need to <u>know about</u> or <u>remember</u> in order to support this business condition or circumstance?"

   The purpose of this question is to discover what data is needed to support the *business event*. To then find the data, you need to do the following:

2. **Look and listen for nouns.** Start by looking in the *business event* statement itself. It will consist of at least a verb and a noun or more. The nouns in the

business event statement are usually Objects, as long as they consist of two or more data items.

3. **Listen for nouns with "substance".** An Object in a business model must consist of at least two data items. Less is just a data attribute. For example, would the noun **CUSTOMER** need several data items to describe it? Would we need to know the *customer's name*, *address*, *phone number*, etc.? If so – and if there are at least two such attributes and characteristics – then we have an Object. If not, then we just have an attribute that belongs to some other Object.

It follows that all nouns are not Objects. Some are just data attributes that belong to and describe Objects. Others are full Objects. To know the difference, you must determine if the piece of data, the noun, can be further decomposed. If you can't further decompose it, it's a data attribute. If you can, it's an Object.

4. **Identify data attributes by listening for nouns that are not Objects.**
Sometimes we just don't know where a data item belongs, mainly because we haven't yet attributed enough data to create a suitable target Object. When a client mentions a series of nouns that are clearly data items and not Objects, but are also undoubtedly related – such as *customer name*, *address*, *phone number* – then we "roll up" a group of related data items to form a new Object that hasn't yet been formed.

???
Data Attributes
• customer name
• customer address
• phone number

5. **Ask the Inclusion Question (for Objects).** For every Object that participates in a *business event* ask the following question:

> **"If I know about {the OBJECT} what will it enable us to do that we could not do if we didn't know about it?"**

6. **Ask the Exclusion Question (for Objects).** For every Object in a *business event* ask the following question:

> **"If we do not know about {the OBJECT} what will it prevent us from doing that we must be able to do?"**

It's also important to recognize that, so far, we have dealt with the issue of populating an Object with data (data attribution) only at the intuitive level. We have not yet dealt at all with the principles of *normalization* and data attribution; i.e., how to find the right home (in an Object) for data items, and how do we do so without redundancy? So, we'll look at that now, with an eye to ease of understanding and simplicity.

2.3 Normalization – What is This?

During business system analysis, information that is relevant to the project must be identified, organized and documented. This process of data discovery, data allocation and organization is called *data normalization*. Contrary to popular uninformed opinion, this must be done to ensure complete and accurate business requirements. But, also contrary to popular misguided opinion, this doesn't have to take forever in the context of business requirements analysis. Nor does it have to be a technical exercise.

The purpose of normalization is to structure data in such a way as to eliminate all forms of redundancy and, ultimately, to allow the processing of the data – in a database structure – without inconsistencies or errors. This means that we have to make sure that any single data item (*customer name*, for example) is maintained in one place only, while being available everywhere it is needed. But, this sounds technical, so why would we care?

Many technical specialists would argue that you shouldn't care; that worrying about data and its *normalization* is the job of database designers. They would argue that you, as a non-technical analyst doing business requirements elicitation, don't need to know a thing about database design (and they are right); nor do you need to know anything about data modeling (again, in the technical sense, they're right). They will tell you that all the technical aspects of data belong in the domain of the database experts. And, of course, they are right.

So, why do you care?

When data is properly attributed to their Objects, and redundancies eliminated, you will then be able to ask highly focused, non-abstract questions of your clients and subject-matter experts. All the questions that you need to ask about their business requirements come from the data (after all, it is data that gives them the information they need from their systems). If the data is just a collection of 'stuff', then it is very difficult to ask meaningful questions. On the other hand, if the data is well organized and non-redundant, you will be able to ask the SMEs very specific and in-context questions about their business requirements, based on the data they need. To be able to find the data, you have to know how to identify it and attribute it properly to Objects. That's *data attribution*. You also have to eliminate the redundancies and data that are hiding behind aliases. That's *data normalization*.

When you allocate data items to Objects, and those Objects are partitioned well, you will achieve the level of detail necessary for good, precise questions for your SMEs, rather than vaguer questions that come from general knowledge. That old saying, *"the devil's in the details"* can be put to rest because proper data attribution and data normalization take the devilish complexity out of finding the questions to ask your clients and SMEs.

A full study of *data normalization* could be an academic endeavor that makes all your other studies pale by comparison. It is not for the weak-of-heart. Thousands of mostly incomprehensible tomes have been written about this subject. Nor would such a study be all that productive. As a non-technical analyst who does business analysis, you need to be able to do it, but you don't necessarily need to explain to everyone what it is and how it works in all its theoretical finery.

To help you overcome the unnecessary technical burden imposed by formal *data normalization*, I have devised a set of five simple rules that – if you follow all of them all the time – will enable you to achieve sufficiently normalized data attribution and well-partitioned Objects, as part of your business requirements analysis.

What this means to you is (a) really good attribution of data to Objects; (b) no redundancy; and, (c) Objects that are ready for inclusion in the **Business Rules Table** so you can find and ask the detailed questions you have to ask your SMEs. We will explore the Business Rules Table in the next section of the book (Part 3).

2.4 The 5 Business Data Rules

No redundancy whatsoever is the key to success with data. Follow these rules and you will never look back.

Business Data Rule # 1

■ **Attribute the data item to the Object it describes best, and to no other Object.**

When we speak with our clients and subject-matter experts to determine their business requirements, we hear all kinds of nouns to describe the business. Some of these nouns are Objects. These Objects, in turn, consist of *other nouns* to describe their content.

Those other nouns that describe an Object's content are data items that must be properly attributed to the right Objects. We call this *finding a home for the data* – or attributing data to an Object. But we don't attribute data items to just any old Object. Each data item must be attributed to the Object *it best describes*. And, of course, each data item can only be attributed to one Object.

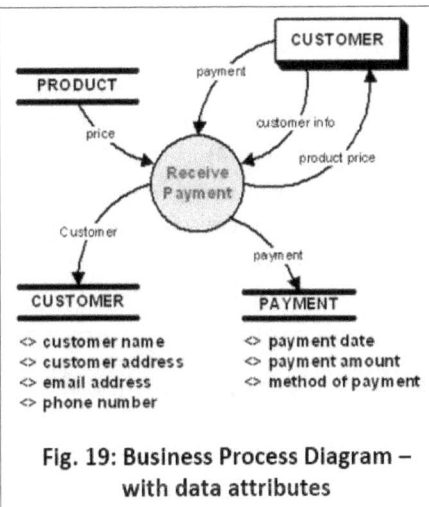

Fig. 19: Business Process Diagram – with data attributes

But sometimes we hear 'stuff' from our clients, and we just don't know where a data item belongs – most likely because we haven't yet set up a named Object to which we can attribute the data we hear. The solution to this situation is to collect seemingly stray data items until we reach critical mass – until a pattern develops. When we have

CUSTOMER
Data Attributes
• customer name
• customer address
• phone number

???
Data Attributes
• customer name
• customer address
• phone number

enough data items that are clearly related – such as *customer name*, *address* and *phone number* – then we "roll up" a group of related data items to form a new Object. This is not usually a big challenge since it only takes two data items to make a distinct Object.

Object: An Object or *entity* is a person, place or thing that a business area or target system needs to know about or remember something about.

While an Object is always a noun, it is distinct from other nouns that are simple data attributes because a business Object:

(1) consists of at least two data attributes, to give it substance;

(2) is essential to the successful operation of the target business area or system (i.e., the Object and its data must be present or the business processes will not be able to do what they are supposed to do); and

(3) is defined by specific **business rules** in specific circumstances.

While it's true that all business Objects must consist of at least two data items to be considered an Object, these Objects can be 'decomposed' to just a single data attribute when designing the database. However, such decomposition comes much later and is not part of business analysis.

Data Attribute: A data attribute is an element of data that is a property of the Object to which it is assigned. A data attribute is defined by a name and description, and eventually represented by a set of values, which may include image and sound. In addition to the business rules that come from the **Business Rules Table** (which we will review in the next chapter) data attributes are required to define what must be remembered or known about each Object. Fig. 20 is an abbreviated example of an Object description (**CUSTOMER**), with governing business rules and data attributes.

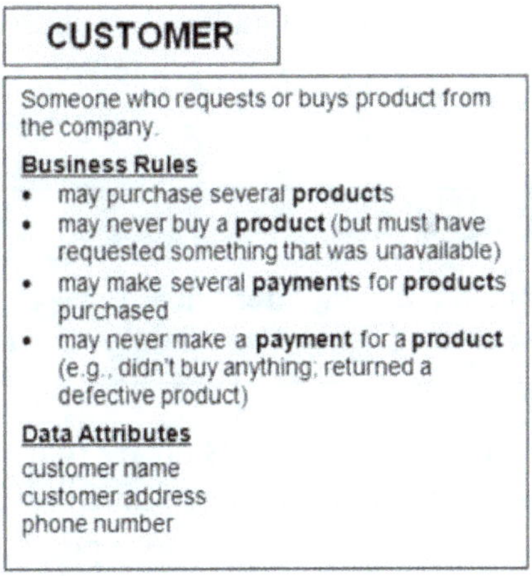

CUSTOMER

Someone who requests or buys product from the company.

Business Rules
- may purchase several **products**
- may never buy a **product** (but must have requested something that was unavailable)
- may make several **payments** for **products** purchased
- may never make a **payment** for a **product** (e.g., didn't buy anything; returned a defective product)

Data Attributes
customer name
customer address
phone number

Fig. 20: Customer Object

Totals and Flags: Totals and 'flags' <u>should</u> not be attributed to Objects, even though it may seem attractive at the time. Neither totals nor 'flags' are real data items; they are the convenient representation of something else. A total can be summed from other data items; therefore, it is redundant. A 'flag' is really a status of some kind, which can usually be determined from some other data attribute such as *time* or *amount*, particularly when the *absence* of data will usually represent a specific status. Flags and totals are therefore redundant and are signs of an early design bias, or a pre-design way of keeping track of something. Flags and totals are usually used to improve database access efficiency. It is best to wait until database design is done to "denormalize" with flags and totals, when all the facts about volumes, data throughput and access requirements have been considered. However, on real-life projects, clients and SMEs often tell me they need this and that 'total' to keep track of accumulations. As an analyst, it's counterproductive to start telling them why we shouldn't do this. Accordingly, I often do record their need for these totals (you need to be seen to be communicating effectively, after all), but I make sure the software engineering team understands they aren't really there, so they can design the appropriate way of determining totals.

Business Data Rule # 2

- **Each Object must have a unique identifier. The unique identifier must not be used as "data".**

Unique Identifier: A unique identifier is an ID that is unique to a specific instance or occurrence of an Object. An Object's 'unique identifier' is also used as a pointer or link to other Objects that participate in a business process to support a *business event*.

An Object's 'unique identifier' is not to be used as data; that's a design choice (a 'how to'), and not a very good one, in my opinion. It is simply a 'unique identifier' or key.

So, why is it important when dealing with business Objects to discuss *unique identifiers* and *keys*? Well, it's so we can all have the same understanding of how Objects are "joined" to support a business process, in such a way that there is no duplication of data.

Business Data Rule # 1 eliminates redundancy; therefore, data items can only appear in one place.

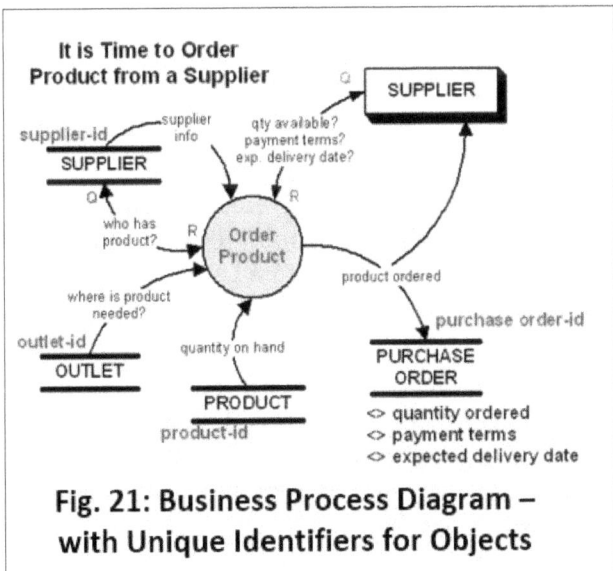

It is Time to Order
Product from a Supplier

supplier-id — supplier info

SUPPLIER

qty available?
payment terms?
exp. delivery date?

SUPPLIER

who has product?

Order Product

product ordered

where is product needed?

outlet-id

OUTLET

quantity on hand

PRODUCT

product-id

purchase order-id

PURCHASE ORDER

◇ quantity ordered
◇ payment terms
◇ expected delivery date

Fig. 21: Business Process Diagram – with Unique Identifiers for Objects

The data items that are needed to fulfill a business process often belong to different Objects. For example, data like *product description* belongs to the Object **PRODUCT**, while data such as *customer name* belongs to the Object **CUSTOMER**.

If a business process needs to be supported by several different Objects, then all the Objects that are needed must be shown as part of the **Business Process Diagram**.

Additionally, each Object must be non-redundant with respect to data. In other words, a specific data item can appear in one and only one Object, and only once, regardless of the name it uses. This means that a specific Object can only contain information about the subject of that Object, and about no other Object. (See **Business Data Rule #1**.)

This, in turn, means that to get information about one or more of the **PAYMENT**s received from a specific **CUSTOMER**, we need to know who the specific **CUSTOMER** is; and the **CUSTOMER** record (Object) must have a pointer or link of some kind that *joins* it to all the **PAYMENT**s we've received from that **CUSTOMER**. (Each **PAYMENT** is distinguished from the other **PAYMENT**s either by the *date of the payment* or by some other data attribute.) Equally true, then, is that if we know the ID of a specific **PAYMENT**, we will be able to find the **CUSTOMER** to whom it belongs.

So, when an Object is shown as being part of a business process, it means that all other Objects (and their data) with which it shares the process can be individually *joined*, based on a pointer or key that connects one Object with another. For example, in Fig. 22, if we know who the **CUSTOMER** is, we can find all the **PAYMENT**s they made; and, if we know the **PRODUCT**, we can find all the **CUSTOMER**s who have bought this **PRODUCT**. Since a unique identifier joins each Object with the right data, we don't have to duplicate information in any Object.

CUSTOMER
Someone who requests or buys product from the company.

Business Rules
- may purchase several **products**
- may never buy a **product** (but must have requested something that was unavailable)
- may make several **payments** for **products** purchased
- may never make a **payment** for a **product** (e.g., didn't buy anything; returned a defective product)

Data Attributes
- customer name
- customer address
- phone number

Unique Identifier
- Customer-ID

Pointers to Related Objects
- Salesperson-ID (mv)
- Outlet-ID (mv)
- Product-ID (mv)
- Payment-ID (mv)

Fig. 22: Object Description

Pointers to Related Objects: A 'Pointer to a Related Object' is an Object's unique identifier contained within another Object. It is often called a "foreign key", meaning it is the key (unique identifier) of an external Object. The "foreign key" provides the ability to find data from other Objects to support the information needs of a specified business process.

The "joining" of Objects in this manner eliminates the need for data repetition or redundancy. "Foreign keys" can be single-valued (i.e., point to just <u>one</u> occurrence of another Object); or they can be multi-valued (i.e., point to <u>several</u> instances of another Object, using the qualifier "**mv**", which means multi-valued or a variable number of instances of the referenced Object). This ratio of occurrences between Objects is determined from the **Business Rules Table**, which in turn specifies the foreign keys needed for the data model, which becomes the prescription for the database design. While developing that data model is not part of business system analysis, the rules required to enable that design come from front-end business analysis.

It is implicit in each **Business Process Diagram** – such as the one in Fig. 23 – that a "relationship" exists between each of the participating Objects. To find the related Objects and data, then, requires that each Object will have a unique identifier and that their respective unique identifiers connect all related Objects.

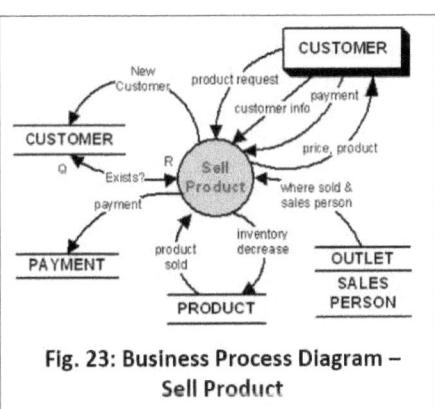

Fig. 23: Business Process Diagram –
Sell Product

Business Data Rule # 3

- **Each Object must have two or more data attributes, other than the unique identifier.**

  (Data items can be part of an Object's data set; and can come from the process that supports the relationship.)

All business Objects must consist of at least two data items for the Object to have substance and therefore exist. If an Object does not have two or more data attributes there will be no way to distinguish an Object – *representing a collection of related data about something specific* – from any other noun that happens to be a single data item. This is the business view. From a database modeling perspective, an Object can be *normalized* to a single data item. But that is not the business view.

We sometimes have Objects that appear to be full of redundancy. Let's look at a typical **PURCHASE ORDER** Object as an example.

Theoretically, the purchase order should, in addition to the data that's specified in Fig. 24 under <u>Data Attributes</u>, also include information such as *product description*, *product cost*, and *supplier name* and *address*.

PURCHASE ORDER

An agreement to purchase product from an accredited supplier, with specific payment and delivery terms prearranged

<u>Business Rules</u>
- is issued to one **supplier** only
- may be for one or many **products**
- may be based on many customer **orders**

<u>Unique Identifier</u>
- purchase order-ID

<u>Data Attributes</u>
- quantity ordered
- payment terms (mv)
- currency type
- expected delivery date
- ...
- ...
- ...

<u>Pointers to Related Objects</u>
- supplier-ID
- product-ID
- outlet-ID (mv)

Fig. 24: Object Description – Foreign Keys and Data

Of course, the **PURCHASE ORDER** Object doesn't have any of this because all of this data is already found in other Objects. In accordance with our **Business Data Rule # 1**, *product description* and *product cost* have already been attributed to the Object **PRODUCT**, and *supplier name* and *address* find their home in **SUPPLIER**. If we attributed this data again to **PURCHASE ORDER** then we would be in violation of **Business Data Rule # 1**; that is, we would have attributed data to more than one Object. And we can't do that.

We can't do that because we already have access to this data by way of *foreign keys* or *pointers to related Objects*. You'll remember that each Object must have a unique identifier (**Business Data Rule # 2**). The identifier for **PURCHASE ORDER** in the diagram above is purchase order-id. You will also recall that a *foreign key* is one Object's unique identifier contained within another Object, as a link. This means that if **PURCHASE ORDER** needs some information that is part of **SUPPLIER**, then **PURCHASE ORDER** will have the unique identifier of **SUPPLIER** as a *foreign key* or link. The same **PURCHASE ORDER** Object (Fig. 24) shows the *Pointers to Related Objects* (foreign keys) it needs to have access to data in the Objects **SUPPLIER** (supplier-id), **PRODUCT** (product-id), and **OUTLET** (outlet-id). Also notice that the **PURCHASE ORDER** may refer to several **OUTLET** records, and it does this by using the convention "mv", meaning multi-valued.

Data often arises from the process that supports a relationship – and that data must be attributed to an Object.

So, what does this mean?

An Object can have data attributed to it that's discovered as part of a supporting process; or, if you like, the data can *arise* out of the process that supports the *business event*. An Object that gets some of its data in this way cannot exist without being dependent on one or more of the other Objects that participate in the relationship. In other words, as shown in Fig. 25, if the **SUPPLIER** Object didn't exist in that process then **PURCHASE ORDER** could not exist either. Why not? Because **PURCHASE ORDER** is dependent on the existence of a **SUPPLIER** record to be able to know the *supplier name* and *address*. Equally, if the **PRODUCT** Object went away so would **PURCHASE ORDER** disappear.

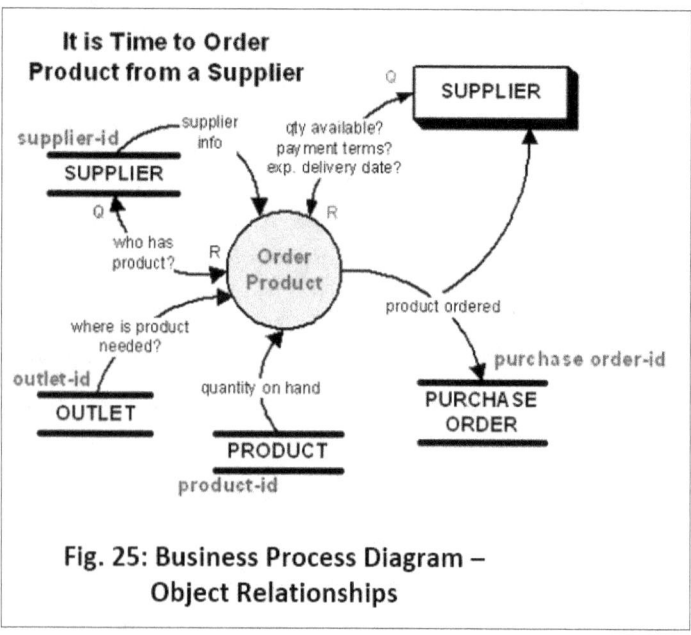

Fig. 25: Business Process Diagram – Object Relationships

The **PURCHASE ORDER** also needs to know what *product* and its *cost* that make up the PO. This means that the **PURCHASE ORDER** is dependent on a specific record (occurrence) of the **PRODUCT** Object.

In the example (Fig. 26), the supporting process generates data such as *quantity ordered*, *payment terms*, *currency type* and *expected delivery date*. None of these data items, required by the **PURCHASE ORDER**, could be found in any other Objects, so they were generated by the supporting business process; which could have been done by a person on the phone, or by some kind of automated process, or a combination of both. <u>How</u> it's done is a solution design issue (we don't have to figure it out now). However, <u>what</u> is needed (the data attributes) is an essential business requirement, which must be determined now.

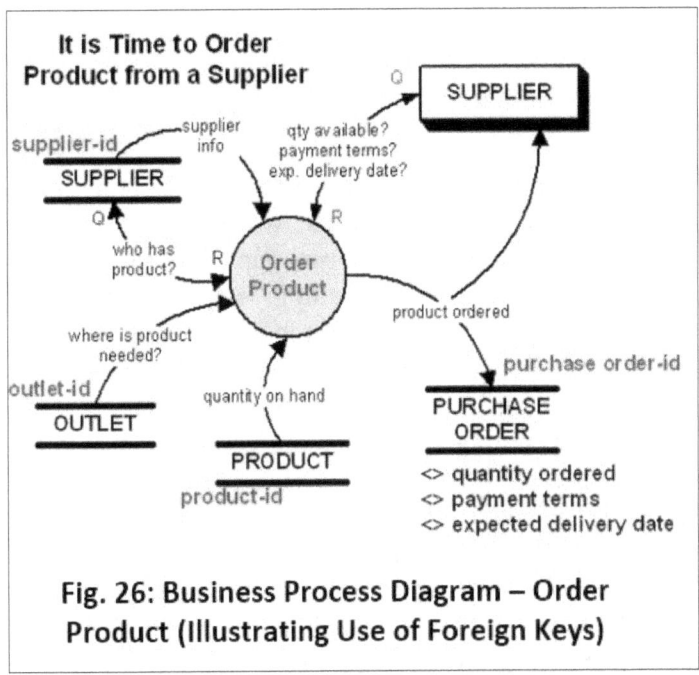

Fig. 26: Business Process Diagram – Order Product (Illustrating Use of Foreign Keys)

An Object that is dependent on other Objects and gets attributed with data in this way is called an *Associative Object*. Most Objects that sound somewhat physical are Associative Objects (such as **PURCHASE ORDER, CONTRACT, POLICY, LICENSE, PERMIT**). It's really not important what it's called (since we never label the type of Object in the documentation anyway) but it is important to know how it got its data. All required data that cannot be found in other Objects that participate in the same process (using *foreign keys*) must *arise from the process* that is being defined, and be attributed to the Associative Object.

Business Data Rule # 4

- **Any data item that is common to all subtypes of an Object must be attributed to that Object's supertype.**

- **Any data item that is attributed to one subtype Object cannot be attributed to any other subtype Object (See Business Data Rule # 1).**

There are times when we need to refer to something globally, and other times when we need to refer to a distinct part of something. For example, an organization with three different kinds of employees (full-time, part-time and contract employees) may refer to all of their employees (i.e., all three different kinds) under one circumstance, or just to one kind of employee (e.g., full-time) under another circumstance. The individual types of employees – **FULL-TIME EMPLOYEE**, **PART-TIME EMPLOYEE** and **CONTRACT EMPLOYEE** – will each have data that is unique only to them. This type of Object is called a *Subtype Object*. The general reference to an "**EMPLOYEE**" will have data that is common to all three different kinds of employees. This type of Object is called a *Supertype Object*.

Subtypes (such as **FULL-TIME EMPLOYEE**) depend on their supertype for existence because each supertype contains data that is common to all of its subtypes, and is necessary to completely describe those subtypes.

Subtypes, however, can be dealt with independently of their supertype. It is usually more precise (and productive) to ask questions of clients and subject-matter experts about the subtype than about the more abstract supertype. For example, when we ask a question about the supertype Object **EMPLOYEE**, we're implying that we include all the different kinds of employees in our questions. On the other hand, when we ask about the subtype Object **FULL-TIME EMPLOYEE**, it's a very specific question that excludes **PART-TIME EMPLOYEE**s and **CONTRACT EMPLOYEE**s. Questions at the subtype level lead to more specific answers than questions at the supertype Object level.

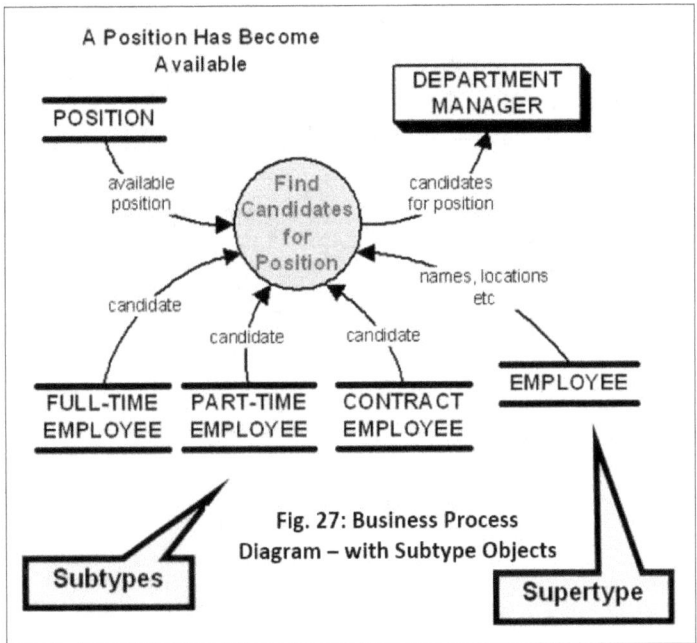

Fig. 27: Business Process Diagram – with Subtype Objects

A subtype Object can also be a supertype to its own subtype.

Creating subtype Objects has a singular business objective: It permits you to ask your clients better, more focused and specific questions.

Business Data Rule # 5

- **When a repeating group of related data (multi-valued data items) is found in a previously defined Object, create a new Object from the multi-valued data items found.**

Sometimes we bury information inside an Object without realizing it. **Business Data Rule # 5** helps us find Objects within Objects. This, in turn, enables us to ask better questions of our clients, which we will see when we review the **Business Rules Table**. Let's look at an example of discovering "characteristic" Objects using the Object **CUSTOMER** (Fig. 28).

To apply Business Data Rule #5 we first determine if there are any data attributes in the Object that are multi-valued (mv), and seem to be part of a common group.

CUSTOMER

Someone who requests or buys product from the company.

Governing Business Rules
- may purchase several **products**
- may never buy a **product** (but must have requested something that was unavailable)
- may make several **payments** for **products** purchased
- may never make a **payment** for a **product** (e.g., didn't buy anything; returned a defective product)

Data Attributes
- customer name
- customer email address
- customer account #
- credit card type (mv)
- credit card # (mv)
- card expiry date (mv)

Unique Identifier
Customer-ID

Pointers to Related Objects
Payment-ID (mv)
Video-ID (mv)

**Fig. 28: Object Description –
Customer**

In the process "**Receive Payment**" (Fig. 29) we find that a customer can pay for a video, potentially at different times. Since we must track how each payment is made, we must include the data attributes _credit card type_, _credit card #_ and _card expiry date_, and each must be multi-valued (mv) to support the different credit cards the customer uses.

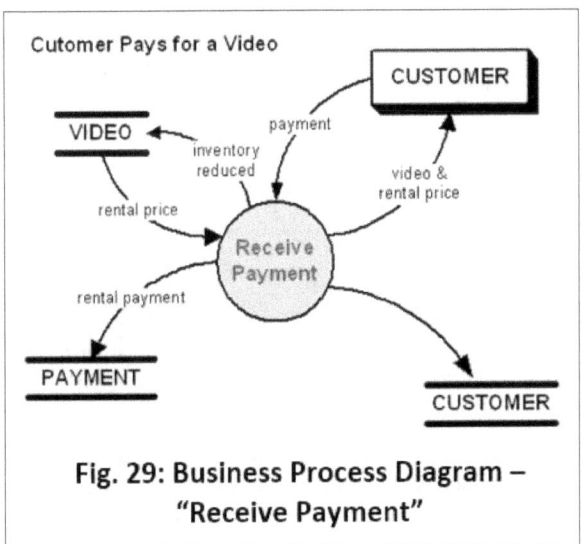

**Fig. 29: Business Process Diagram –
"Receive Payment"**

To apply Business Data Rule # 5, the multi-valued items found in **CUSTOMER** that belong to a common group (_credit card type_, _credit card #_ and _card expiry date_) are removed from the Parent Object (**CUSTOMER**) to establish a new Object (**CREDIT CARD**) that is characteristic of its Parent.

By taking repeating groups of data out of an Object (such as the above _credit card type_, _credit card #_ and _card expiry date_, which are all multi-valued) and creating a new Object with the data, we are able to ask the client more precise and better focused questions (which we'll look at in detail when we get to the **Business Rules Table**, in the next chapter). In this example (Fig. 30), we are now able to ask the client questions about the specific type of payment made by the customer (the credit card), not just the payment in general. This increased granularity gives us better knowledge about the process of paying for the video, and how that payment is made.

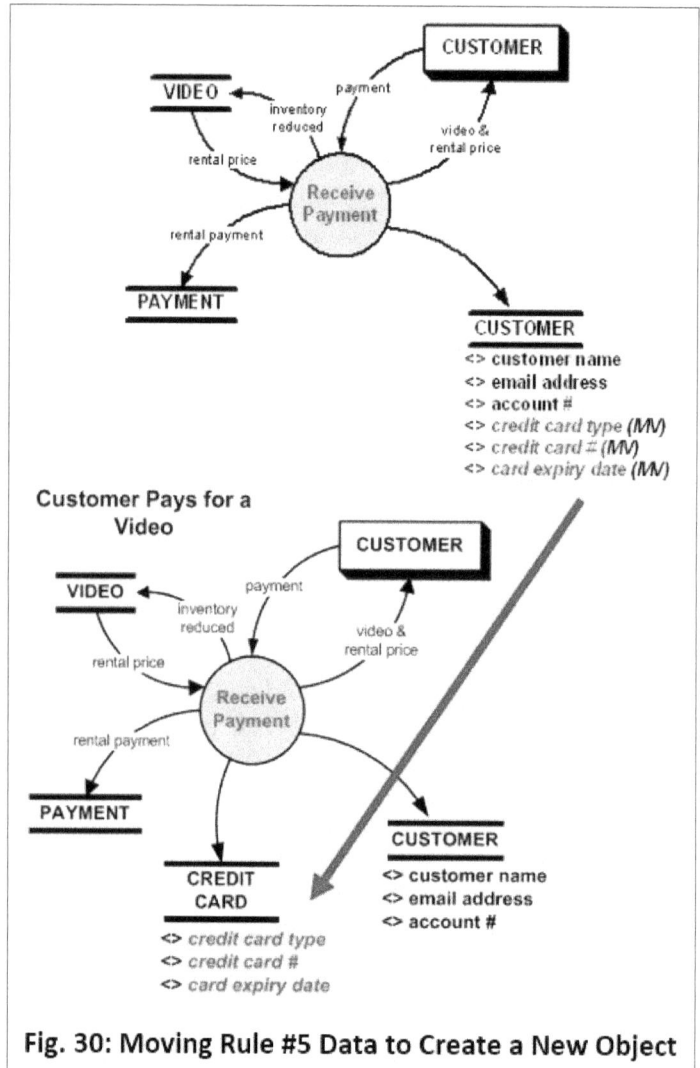

Fig. 30: Moving Rule #5 Data to Create a New Object

Note that the data items we moved from **CUSTOMER** to create the Object **CREDIT CARD** – *credit card type*, *credit card #* and *card expiry date* – are no longer multi-valued when they are used to create the **CREDIT CARD** Object. That's because each Object is seen as a single instance or occurrence of the thing it represents; i.e., it is a single **CREDIT CARD** record. In other words, each **PAYMENT** is made with a single, specific **CREDIT CARD** by the **CUSTOMER**.

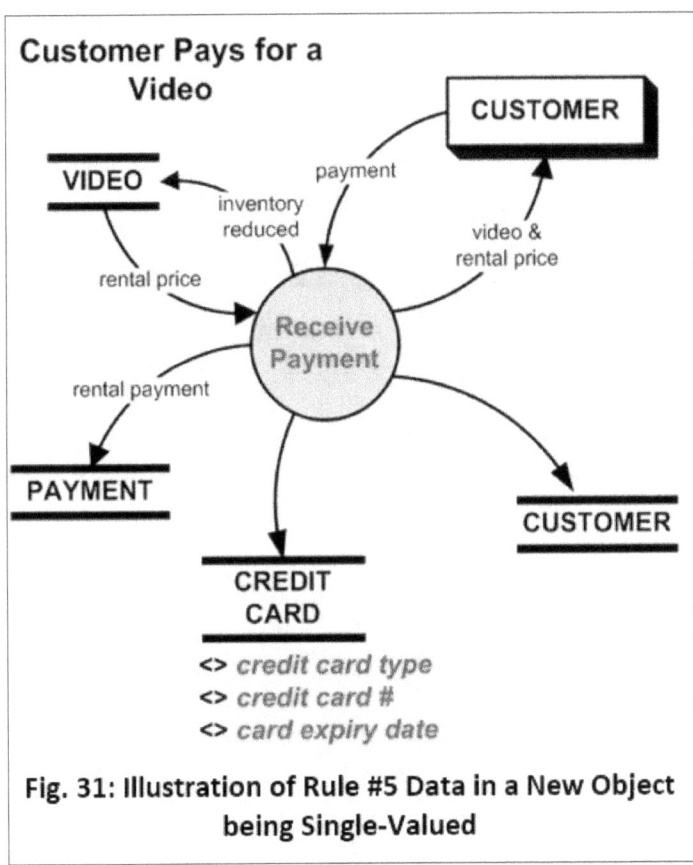

Fig. 31: Illustration of Rule #5 Data in a New Object being Single-Valued

Once you have internalized the **5 Business Data Rules** you will find yourself automatically removing multi-valued groups of data to form new Characteristic

Objects. You will find that you can do this literally as you speak with your clients and first determine the need for the Object (**CREDIT CARD** in this case) and as you discuss the need to know about the customer's payments at different times. Once you have had sufficient practice with this approach to business systems analysis and process modeling you won't spend a lot of time thinking about it, you'll just do it. But you will also miss a few when you're working directly with the client. So, we suggest you carefully review each Object when the client is not around. Then just look for any multi-valued ("mv") group of data that can be pulled out to make a new Characteristic Object. It's that easy. And remember, a group must consist of at least two data attributes (Business Data Rule # 3).

Summary of the Business Data Rules

- **Business Data Rule # 1.** Attribute the data item to the Object it describes best, and to no other Object.

- **Business Data Rule # 2.** Each Object must have a unique identifier. The unique identifier must not be used as "data".

- **Business Data Rule # 3.** Each Object must have two or more data attributes, other than the unique identifier.

- **Business Data Rule # 4.** Any data item that is common to all subtypes of an Object must be attributed to that Object's supertype. Any data item that is attributed to one subtype Object cannot be attributed to another subtype Object.

- **Business Data Rule # 5.** When a repeating group of related data (multi-valued items) is found in a previously defined Object, create a new Object from the multi-valued data items found.

2.5 Do You Really Need That Data Item?

As we discover Objects that are needed to support different business processes, we also find the nouns that are single data items, and we need to find a home for them. We attribute these data items to the right Objects by following the 5 Business Data Rules. But, data shouldn't be automatically accepted as necessary to support a business area or process just because someone mentions the data. In many cases data is included – just because it has always been there. The data item could be the legacy of an old system, but how do we find out if we still need the data that clients and subject-matter experts sometimes talk about?

Earlier, we discussed how to apply the *Inclusion* and *Exclusion Questions (for Objects)*. We can do exactly the same thing with data items.

Ask the <u>Inclusion</u> Question (for Data).

Often when discussing a business process, different data items are mentioned by the client, but it's sometimes difficult to tell if all those data items are really necessary. How can we tell? One way to determine if a data item should be included is to ask the following question:

"If we know about {<u>the data item</u>} **what will it <u>enable</u> us to do that we could not do if we didn't know about it?"**

Let's look at an example using the *business event* "**It is Time to Deposit a Customer Payment to a Bank Account**".

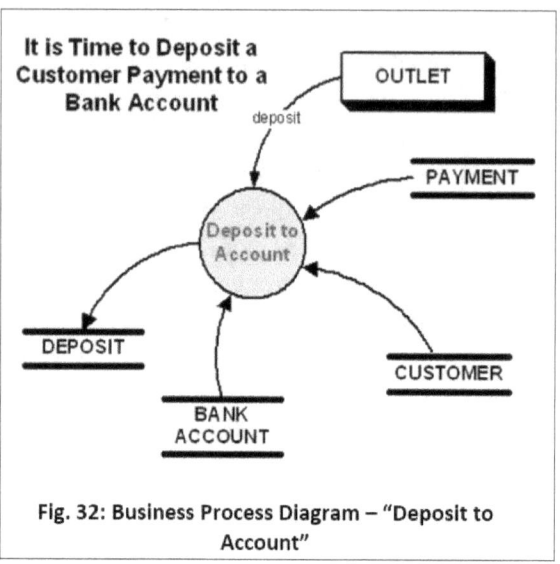

Fig. 32: Business Process Diagram – "Deposit to Account"

Our subject-matter experts tell us that we need to keep track of the **PAYMENT**s that are **DEPOSIT**ed. We also need to know into which **BANK ACCOUNT** the payments are deposited; and, since there are many customers from coast-to-coast, we must know which **CUSTOMER** the deposited payment belongs to so we have a proper audit trail.

As we listen to our client we are able to identify each of these as proper Objects (they all are nouns) which we recognized to consist of two or more data attributes ... things we want to know about them. One of the data attributes belonging to the Object **DEPOSIT** is *date of deposit*. If we weren't sure this item was really needed, the first question

---

DEPOSIT

Data Attributes

- date of deposit
- name of depositor

would be, *is this really a necessary data item?* How can we tell? To find out let's restate the "Data Inclusion" question.

"If we know about {the date of deposit} **what will it enable us to do that we could not do if we didn't know about it?"**

In this example, *date of deposit* will allow us to reconcile our deposits against statements provided by the bank. Of course, that begs the question *do we want to reconcile deposits?* Is it within the scope of the project? Only our client knows for sure. If the answer is... *yes, reconciliation is within the scope of the project...* then we definitely need to know about the *date of deposit*.

DEPOSIT
Data Attributes
• date of deposit
• name of depositor

Also, if reconciliation is within the scope of the project we must ask the question, *have we identified a business event for reconciliation yet?* If not, then we must add a new *business event*, **"It is Time to Reconcile Bank Statement"**.

Ask the Exclusion Question (for Data).

There is another side of the 'Data Inclusion' question. Sometimes it makes more sense to try to take something away than to imagine it being added. This is the same as the 'Data Inclusion' test, but we're just coming at it from the other direction. In this case, the question we ask is stated as follows:

"If we do not know about {the data item} **what will it prevent us from doing that we must be able to do?"**

Let's use the same example as before, "**It is Time to Deposit Customer Payment to a Bank Account**".

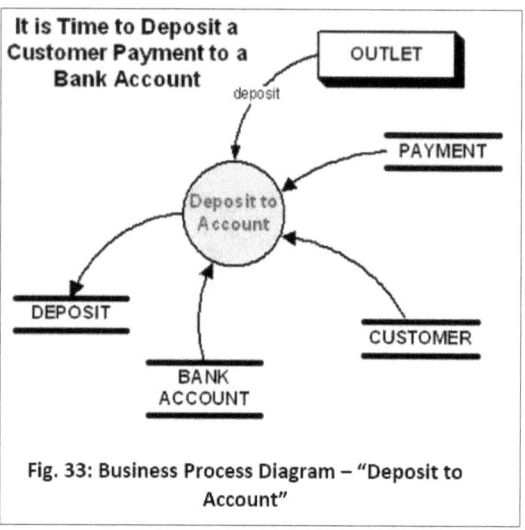

Fig. 33: Business Process Diagram – "Deposit to Account"

"**If we <u>do not</u> know about** {<u>the date of deposit</u>} **what will it <u>prevent</u> us from doing that we must be able to do?**"

In this example (as in the previous one) it will prevent us from reconciling our deposits against statements received from the bank. Once again we have the same questions, _do we want to reconcile deposits_? Is it within the scope of the project? If the answer is... _yes, reconciliation is within the scope of the project_... then we must have the _date of deposit_.

As with the 'Data Inclusion' test, we must add a new _business event_ to be able to deal with "**It is Time to Reconcile Bank Statement**".

People have different views of things. That's why we have developed the 'Inclusion' and 'Exclusion' tests, so your clients will have the opportunity of seeing the subject from their own point of view – whether something is enabled, or it is prevented – which helps to make the questions clear to them; not just to the analysts, but to the client. It's always a matter of perspective. Some people are more comfortable answering questions that exclude rather than include. It's probably that left-brain vs. right-brain thing.

Ask the <u>Inclusion</u> or <u>Exclusion</u> Questions (for Reports).

This is one of my personal favorites.

Here we are, well into the 21st century, but so many people still want to see reports being the primary output of systems. A report, of course, if a solution to some question – it's a *how* are we going to provide certain information, in some context.

Rather than trying to tell your clients or SMEs that true business analysis doesn't address "how" something is done (such as issuing a report) but focuses on what is required to meet a need – which really means the essential data, not how it is delivered – it's best to find out the reason the client needs the report.

If the client says, *"We need a sales report for widgets in the northeast region"* we can ask either or both of the Inclusion and Exclusion Questions, as follows:

"If we <u>do not</u> know about {<u>the sales results for the northeast region</u>} what will it <u>prevent</u> us from doing that we must be able to do?"

Or ….

"If we know about {the sales results for the northeast region} **what will it enable us to do that we could not do if we didn't know about it?"**
The client's answer to either question can then be translated into a *business event* – a situation or circumstance that the system has to deal with.

There you have it: An effective way of using a request for a report to determine what the real *business event* may be.

Part 3.
The Business Rules Table

The single most difficult issue for any analyst when doing requirements elicitation and analysis has always been finding the right questions to ask clients and subject-matter experts (SMEs). The analyst's quandry has always been, *How do I know what I should ask these people? What should my first question be? And what should I ask next?*

Every business and system analysis methodology has always lacked this fundamental foundation – a method to find the exact, in-context questions to ask clients and SMEs. The only way we can be assured of the completeness of any business requirements specification is to somehow know that we have asked all the right questions, and none have been missed. Anything less makes not a business system specification, but a business *speculation*. Business requirements analysis isn't horseshoes. *"Close is good enough"* just isn't acceptable for the sophisticated, integrated, expensive business systems we need to have today.

The Kinds of Questions

Agile business analysis means nothing if we can't find all the correct questions to ask our stakeholders. It's not "agile" to leave unasked, and unanswered, questions on the floor. Therefore, to be able to start and finish business requirements analysis for any project, all of the following questions must be answered or resolved.

1. **How do I find all the right questions to ask?** How do I quickly find all the questions to ask our clients and SMEs? How do I know what the questions should be? (The operative words here are *find*, *all* and *quickly*.)

2. **How do I know all the right questions have been asked?** How do I find unanswered questions? How do I find the ones no one ever seems to find, or the ones we promised to come back to later and need to keep track of? How do I know we're done? How do I know we have found all the questions that need to be asked? (In other words, how can I know what I don't know?)

3. **How do I find the real limits of the project?** How do I find the questions that determine the real scope of the project? How do I prevent 'scope creep' during the project? How do I avoid surprises? (Or, how can I turn the scope issue into something real rather than trying to pin Jell-O to a wall?)

4. **How do I create a small, understandable and business-focused requirements document that everyone can understand?** How can I put all the related documentation in the same place, without redundancy, so I can find it again? How do I make the documentation brief, event-based, and not like a Victorian novel, so we can easily maintain it and find elements? How can I write it in business language, and not base it on the technology we're implementing? How can I make sure it focuses on the business and not on the technology solution? (And, how can we

release and distribute in an "agile" fashion using modern media?)

5. **How do I describe data access requirements based on the business needs?** If we need a database design, how can I quickly determine the data accesses required by the business needs, so database designers don't have to go out and reinvent the business wheel? (And how can I, as a non-technical analyst – and not a database designer – do this magic?)

3.1 How to Find the Questions to Ask

All of the questions listed above can be answered and resolved by using the questions outlined in Part 2, the *Inclusion / Exclusion Questions*, and the **Business Rules Table**, which we will discuss below.

The **Business Rules Table** (BRT) is a question generator. It requires a specific syntax – a *language of structure* – so we can ask questions of clients and SMEs. This syntax eliminates personal and subjective evaluations of whether a question (or answer) is a 'good' one. All BRT-generated questions, and all answers from clients, have an equal value. This means we never have to be concerned with someone else's intuitive understanding.

- The **Business Rules Table** enables the analyst to easily identify and structure all questions to be asked about the business domain, in the context of specific business processes.

- The **Business Rules Table** enables the analyst to write a clear statement for the desired business policy, in plain language, in the context of a specific business process.

- The **Business Rules Table** enables the analyst to know where to document the client's answer, and to know where to find the answer in the future.

- The **Business Rules Table** enables the business analyst to find *business events* (i.e., conditions, situations and circumstances) the client did not recognize to be part of the project's scope, and therefore the supporting business processes that would otherwise be missed.

- The **Business Rules Table** enables the analyst to know when there are no more questions to ask the client about the project's business requirements.

The resulting documentation, written in plain and simple business language, can be easily read and evaluated by the client or subject-matter experts. The succinctness of the documentation enables SMEs to evaluate individual business processes and to determine if any new processes and data effectively contribute to the organization's mission, goals and direction.

Governing business rules, which come from the questions generated by the **Business Rules Table**, are the rules or policies that govern the existence or behavior of {the Object we are questioning}, in the context of a specific business process. Everything we learn about an Object is documented as a set of rules that govern the client's business, in a specific circumstance. These rules become the key part of the business requirements specification. They represent functionality and required (or denied) behavior in a specific situation.

Each Object that is part of a process supporting a *business event* (Fig. 34) becomes part of a matrix called the **Business Rules Table**. The symbols used in the BRT (see Fig. 35) are shorthand notation for specific answers to the questions that are asked. Although the BRT contains the shorthand notation, the actual context-specific rules are documented in plain language, using declarative statements.

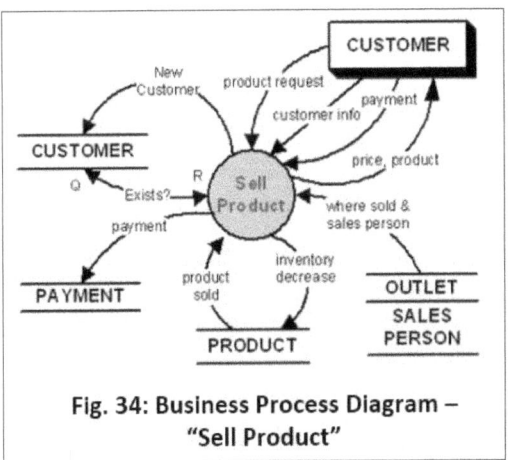

Fig. 34: Business Process Diagram – "Sell Product"

Symbols used in the **Business Rules Table** to symbolize this shorthand, also known as *ratio of occurrences* (or cardinality), are shown in Fig. 35.

1	=	One only
N	=	Numerous (more than one)
0	=	None (means "never")
NA	=	Does not apply (= 0 [zero] occurrences)

Fig. 35: Notation for Business Rules Table (BRT)

Using a *language of structure* to ask questions of clients results in business rules specific to a process. These business rules are documented, as declarative statements, also specific to a business process.

From a data perspective, a process can also be seen as a relationship among Objects, behaving in a specific context.

A **Business Rules Table** is produced for each **Business Process Diagram**. An example of the completed **Business Rules Table** for the process "**Sell Product**" is shown in Fig. 36. The business process **"Sell Product"** (see Fig. 34) supports the *business event* "**The Customer Buys a Product**".

BRT	Salesperson	Customer	Outlet	Product	Payment
1 Salesperson		N,0	1,N	N,0	N,0
1 Customer	1,N,0		1,N	1,N,0	1,N,0
1 Outlet	N	N		N	N
1 Product	1,N,0	1,N,0	1,N		1,N,0
1 Payment	1,N	1	1	1,N	

These are the 'Anchor' Objects.

Fig. 36: Business Rules Table (BRT) – "Sell Product"

Business Rules Table questions have a *language of structure* to get good answers. "Good" means nothing less than complete and accurate. Each Object must be queried with three (3) specific questions to uncover all the business rules relevant to the specific process in which it participates, <u>and</u> to be able to find other *business events* required to support the target business area. Below is an example of the type of rules that would result from the table entries shown in Fig. 36 for the Object **SALESPERSON**. The rule notation in Fig. 36 is read from left to right, and translates into the text in Fig. 37. I'll explain how we derive the business rules text.

Each Object is placed in the **Business Rules Table** twice – once as an entry in the row on the left and once in a column at the top. (See the BRT in Fig. 36.) We add Objects to the table only as they are discovered when we determine the Objects necessary to support a business process.

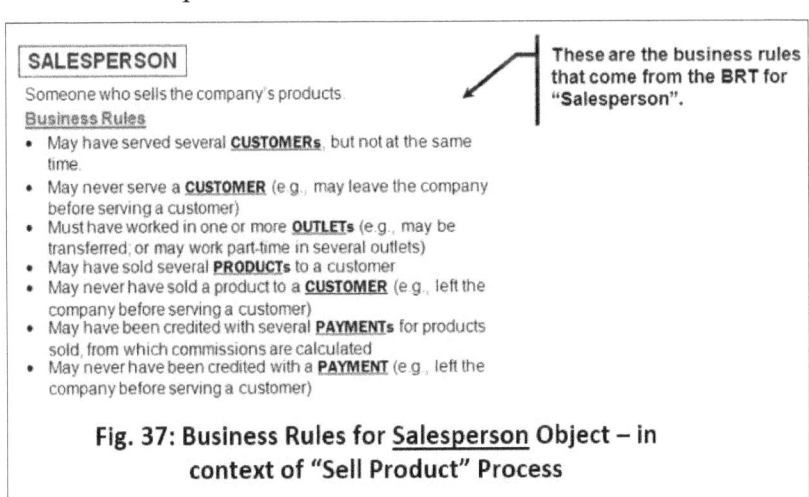

Fig. 37: Business Rules for Salesperson Object – in context of "Sell Product" Process

An Object can intersect or *join* with several other Objects in the table. An Object in this Table must always "join" or intersect with at least one other Object. In some rare cases, a single Object may be the only one in a specific process, which means it has a recursive relationship with itself. When this happens, it meets the rule of always having a relationship or intersection with at least one other Object.

BRT	Salesperson	Customer	Outlet
1 Salesperson			
1 Customer			
1 Outlet			

We start here with the first 'anchor' Object.

Fig. 38: Business Rules Table – Where to Start

We start at the first row on the left with the first Object.

We then ask questions about Objects that appear in a specific **Business Process Diagram**. (We'll visit what the specific questions are in a moment.) We ask our questions of only two Objects at one time ... in binary pairs, if you like. This enables us to ask a series of stable questions and get specific, stable answers.

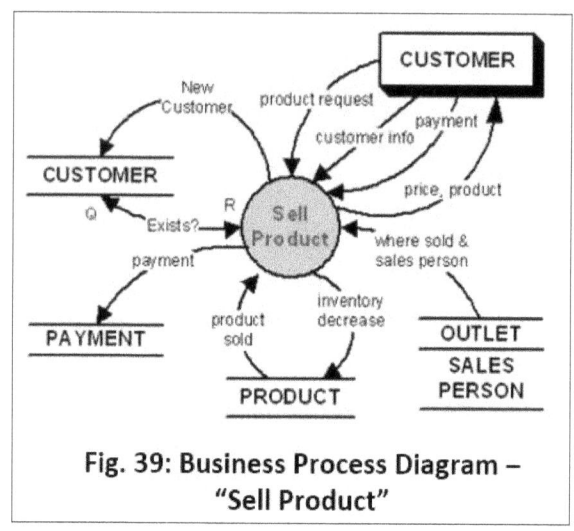

Fig. 39: Business Process Diagram – "Sell Product"

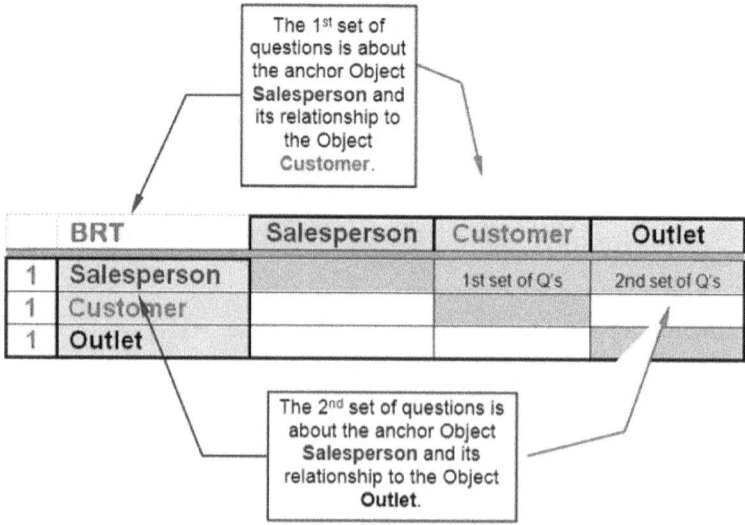

Fig. 40: Business Rules Table (BRT) – Relationship between Objects

So, how does this work? Let's work through an example using just three of the Objects identified in the **Business Process Diagram** for "Sell Product".

From the process "**Sell Product**", place the Objects in the **Business Rules Table** – once in a row on the left, and once in a column across the top. Place the number "**1**" in front of each anchor Object. This will help us focus on a single instance of the anchor Object when we ask the questions that arise from this table. (I did not place all of the Objects from the "**Sell Product**" process into the BRT, just to conserve some space.)

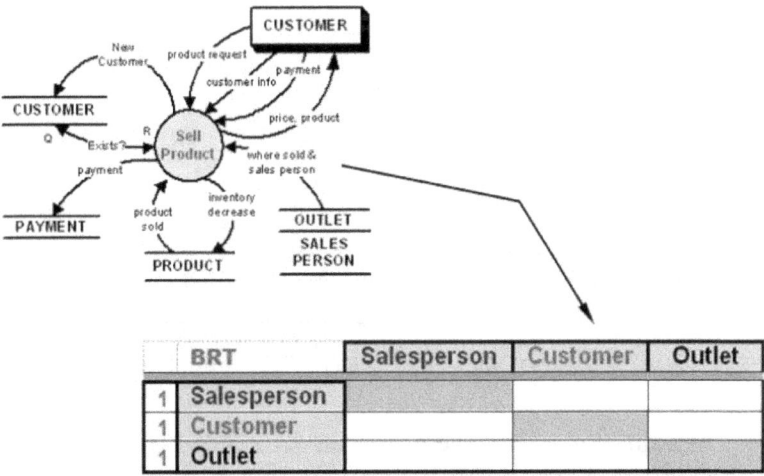

Fig. 41: Business Rules Table (BRT) – "Sell Product"

We start with the first anchor Object, and we structure the questions as follows:

Structure: "For a single, specific {<u>anchor OBJECT</u>} how many {<u>intersecting OBJECTs</u>} might {<u>verb construct</u>}?"

Let's put that into an English-language structure we can all understand.

"For a single, specific <u>SALESPERSON</u> how many <u>CUSTOMER</u>s might he or she <u>serve</u>?"

The questions that come from this table (see Fig. 42) must always be put into a context. The context is the verb you chose. For example, what do salespersons do in the "**Sell Product**" process? They **sell to** or **serve** customers. In this example, then, the context must be something like the verb ***to serve*** or ***to sell***. I have chosen ***to serve*** since it seems easier to work with. Words like "associated" or "related" should never be used since they are far too abstract and only have meaning to the person using them.

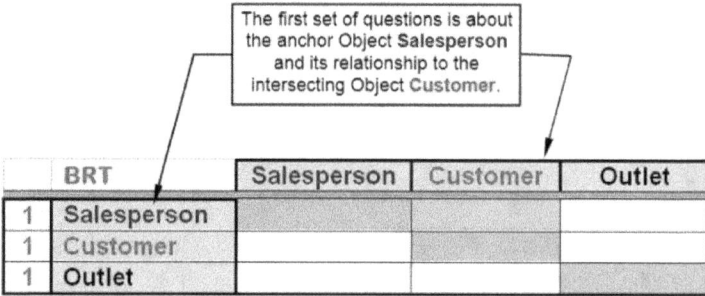

Fig. 42: Business Rules Table (BRT) – First Set of Questions

This initial question we ask is only intended to help us focus our thinking. Never attempt to answer this first, general question. It's just a mental placeholder, so we can get on with the more specific questions. We immediately follow this initial question with three very specific questions, each soliciting a clear and unambiguous answer.

QUESTION # 1:

Structure: "Could the {anchor OBJECT} {relationship context verb} just one {intersecting OBJECT}?"

Or, in plain English:

"Could the SALESPERSON serve just one CUSTOMER?"

QUESTION # 2:

Structure: "Could the {anchor OBJECT} {relationship context verb} several {intersecting OBJECTs}?"

Or, in plain English:

"Could the SALESPERSON serve several CUSTOMERs?"

QUESTION # 3:

Structure: "Might the {anchor OBJECT} never {relationship context verb} any {intersecting OBJECTs} at all?"

Or, in plain English:

"Might the SALESPERSON never serve any CUSTOMERs at all?"

So far, we have a total of four questions, except that the initial "placeholder" question doesn't require an answer.

PLACEHOLDER QUESTION:

"For a single, specific SALESPERSON how many CUSTOMERs might he or she serve?" (Do not wait for the answer.)

This is followed immediately by three very specific, structured questions, each requiring a response from the client or subject matter expert.

QUESTION # 1: "Could the SALESPERSON serve just <u>one</u> CUSTOMER?"

QUESTION # 2: "Could the SALESPERSON serve <u>several</u> CUSTOMERs?"

QUESTION # 3: "Might the SALESPERSON never serve <u>any</u> CUSTOMERs at all?"

BRT		Salesperson	Customer	Outlet
1	**Salesperson**		?	
1	Customer			
1	Outlet			

Fig. 43: Business Rules Table (BRT) – Questions in the Intersection Cell

Each of these questions is asked in what we call a client-interactive "requirements *discovery* session". Discovery sessions with subject-matter experts are very similar to technical JAD sessions, but *discovery* sessions focus entirely on the business requirements and not on system solutions or design. **J**oint **A**pplication **D**esign (or **D**evelopment) is a session in which subject-matter experts and system developers interact to determine <u>system</u> functionality and output. In business discovery sessions, answers to questions are captured by an expert scribe, based on the **Business Rules Table**s for each Business Process Diagram.

Let's play through the answers to our questions – we'll make up some answers along the way, pretending subject-matter experts are present – and populate the **Business Rules Table** with the values representing our made-up answers. From these answers we'll also generate plain-language text that documents the rules in Objects.

Start with the **PLACEHOLDER QUESTION: "For a single, specific SALESPERSON how many CUSTOMERs might he or she serve?"** But don't wait for an answer. Immediately go on with the three follow-on questions.

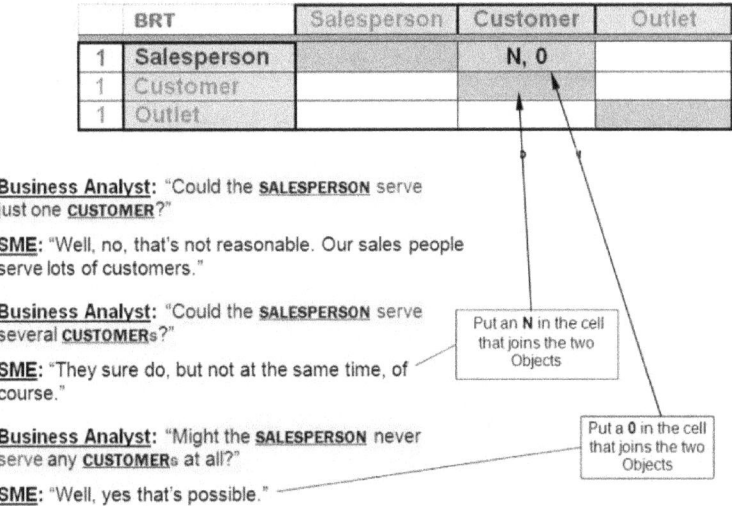

Business Analyst: "Could the SALESPERSON serve just one CUSTOMER?"

SME: "Well, no, that's not reasonable. Our sales people serve lots of customers."

Business Analyst: "Could the SALESPERSON serve several CUSTOMERs?"

SME: "They sure do, but not at the same time, of course."

Business Analyst: "Might the SALESPERSON never serve any CUSTOMERs at all?"

SME: "Well, yes that's possible."

Fig. 44: Business Rules Table (BRT) – Questions to Answer: Salesperson-Customer

You will recall that earlier we reviewed the notation we use to record the ratio of occurrences between Objects. Ratio of occurrences, or cardinality, specifies how many instances (or occurrences) of an intersecting Object there are for a single anchor Object. Now, by itself, that's not very interesting information, and it doesn't seem to have much to do with business requirements analysis. But the moment we put that into the context of a business process, then we've defined the nature of the relationship between the intersecting Objects, and we can define the rules of that relationship, as specified by our subject-matter experts. As an analyst, you don't have to agree with the rules the SMEs specify; but you do have to accept that they know more about their business than we do. I've repeated the notation so we can all work from the same page.

1	=	One only
N	=	Numerous (more than one)
0	=	None (means "never")
NA	=	Does not apply (= 0 [zero] occurrences)

Fig. 45: Business Rules Table (BRT) – Notation

By revisiting the 3rd Question we find that the SME gave us a technically correct but not very enlightening answer:

Business Analyst: "Might the **SALESPERSON** never serve any **CUSTOMER**s at all?"

SME: "Well, yes that's possible."

With this answer, we enter a "**0**" in the Business Rules Table cell (at the intersection of **SALESPERSON** and **CUSTOMER**) but we must go on to a follow-on question.

Business Analyst's Follow-on Question:
"Under what circumstances might that be true – that they might never serve a customer?"

SME: "Well, they could leave the company before serving their first customer."

Whenever there is a "never" response from a client, such as above, you must always ask one additional question – "**Under what circumstances might that be**

true?" This is the final Question and is only asked when the client responds to the 3rd Question with "never".

Each of the rules you have now discovered must also be documented in plain language. This isn't difficult, especially since you have already selected the context (verb construct) that you will use. Let's review the questions (and answers) in our example.

Business Analyst's 1st Question: "Could the **SALESPERSON** serve just one **CUSTOMER**?"

SME: "Well, no, that's not reasonable. Our sales people serve lots of customers."

Since the answer was "no" then there is nothing to add to the **Business Rules Table** and nothing to write up as the business rule.

Business Analyst's 2nd Question: "Could the **SALESPERSON** serve several **CUSTOMER**s?"

SME: "They sure do, but not at the same time, of course."

With this answer, we now know that a salesperson may serve many customers, since serving none is not a reasonable scenario. With this answer, we enter **"N"** in the cell that joins **SALESPERSON** with **CUSTOMER**.

BRT		Salesperson	Customer	Outlet
1	Salesperson		N	
1	Customer			
1	Outlet			

Fig. 46. Business Rules Table (BRT) Notation – Salesperson-Customer

We then write the rule in plain language under the 'anchor' Object (**SALESPERSON**). The rule can be written as *"may have served several customers, but not at the same time"*. When we use 'may' as in "may have served several customers" we are also implying the salesperson "may not have served several customers". Therefore, before we choose 'may' instead of 'must' it's important to know the answer to the next question, since the words we choose to write our rules do have precise meanings.

SALESPERSON

Someone who sells the company's products.

Business Rules
- May have served several **CUSTOMER**s, but not at the same time
- May never serve a **CUSTOMER**

Data Attributes
- salesperson name
- salesperson address
- salesperson phone # (mv)
- salesperson fax #
- salesperson email address (mv)

Unique Identifier
Salesperson-ID

Fig. 47: Object Business Rules

Business Analyst's 3rd Question: Might the **SALESPERSON** never serve any **CUSTOMER**s at all?"

SME: "Well, yes they could."

With this answer, we also place a **"0"** (zero) in the cell that joins **SALESPERSON** with **CUSTOMER**. The rule can be written as *"may never serve a customer"*.

	BRT	Salesperson	Customer	Outlet
1	**Salesperson**		**N, 0**	
1	Customer			
1	Outlet			

Fig. 48: Business Rules Table (BRT) Notation – Salesperson-Customer

Whenever we get a "never" response to this 3rd question we must ask a fourth follow-on question to determine the condition that makes it true.

Business Analyst's 4th Question: "Under what circumstances might that be true?"

SME: "Well, they could leave the company before serving their first customer."

In this case, because we got a "never" response to the 4th question, we must qualify the business rule we previously recorded. In this case we take the original rule (*"may never serve a customer"*) and add *"e.g., may leave the company before serving a customer."* As with the original statement, this rule is allocated to the anchor Object **SALESPERSON**.

Whenever a "never" response is given by a client, they must support the "never" condition with an example (or several). In turn, you must determine if the circumstances identified in the example is <u>a</u> *<u>business event</u> that has not yet been included* in the project's scope... and if so, is it in-scope or out-of-scope?

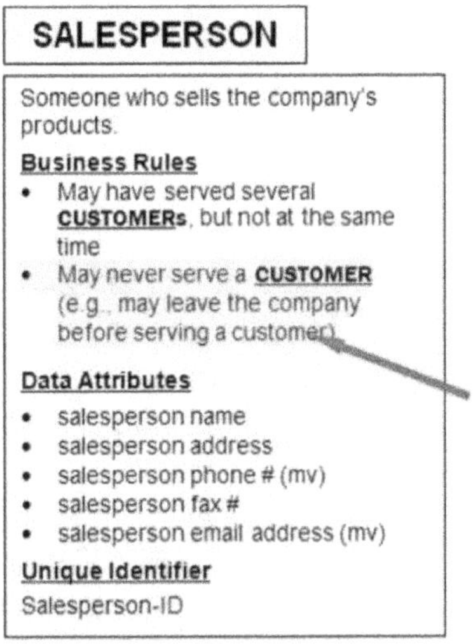

SALESPERSON

Someone who sells the company's products.

Business Rules
- May have served several **CUSTOMERs**, but not at the same time
- May never serve a **CUSTOMER** (e.g., may leave the company before serving a customer)

Data Attributes
- salesperson name
- salesperson address
- salesperson phone # (mv)
- salesperson fax #
- salesperson email address (mv)

Unique Identifier
Salesperson-ID

Fig. 49: Object Business Rules with example of "never" response to 4th BRT Question

In the example we are using, we state that the salesperson may leave the company. The question you must therefore ask the client is, *"Is this something – the salesperson may leave the company before serving a customer – that we want to keep track of?"*

The simple fact that a SME mentioned the example – stimulated by our question – forces us to consider its inclusion. If the SME's answer is *"yes, it's something we want to keep track of"* we must add it to our parking lot of *business events* that make up the project's scope – perhaps listed as "**The Employee Terminates**" (i.e., quits, dies, retires). If the client's answer is *"no, it's not part of the scope"* then we won't include it. (But, we will make a list of *business events* found to be out-of-scope as well. This gives us a good audit or management trail.) However, it's not usual for a SME to use an example of a situation that could arise, and then say it's not something they want to know about. But, in the end, it's either in or it's out.

I have found it is easier to get a response when asking if "we want to keep track of" something, rather than "Is this within the project's scope?" Earlier, we discussed how all systems just keep track of things. (If you don't keep track of something, you can't know about it.) Therefore, if the client wants to "keep track of" something, it means it's inside scope. This is also why so many projects are called "ABC Tracking Project".

Two *business event* lists should be maintained – one for **In-Scope Business Events** and another for **Out-of-Scope Business Events**. This enables us to keep track of those *business events* that were discussed but determined to be out-of-scope. The out-of-scope *business events* could become in-scope on a future project. By keeping track we're also able to answer questions such as, "did you discuss ....?"

The 4th BRT Question is a primary method used to discover *business events* that are within a project's scope. That's why it is so important to listen carefully to what clients and subject-matter experts have to say, especially to their "never" answers, and to get the circumstances that make the "never" responses true.

This procedure of asking 3 or 4 specific questions (which we simply call the 'BRT Questions') is repeated for all the Objects that intersect with the anchor Object **SALESPERSON**. After we have finished asking questions of all the Objects that have a relationship with **SALESPERSON** – specific to a process – then we go on to the next anchor Object, which is **CUSTOMER** in our example.

	BRT	Salesperson	Customer	Outlet
1	Salesperson		N, 0	1, N
1	Customer			
1	Outlet			

These are the 'Anchor' Objects.

Fig. 50: Business Rules Table (BRT) – Relationship between Objects

Because there are three very specific questions (and sometimes a fourth) you will never fumble trying to figure out what the questions should be or what comes next. You will find the 'BRT Questions' procedure to be very fast and effective. And you will find that your clients relate to these questions very well. They sometimes struggle to answer, but that's because the questions are so specific and call for a precise answer.

Many interesting discussions and policies come out of these questions.

Where do we put the rules? All rules are allocated to and documented under the Object that is the 'anchor' Object in the question.

And when we're all done we have all kinds of business rules attributed to all the Objects that we need to support a specific process. Our limited example, **SALESPERSON**, would look something like the entry in Fig. 51. We will play through a more complete example later.

SALESPERSON

Someone who sells the company's products.

Business Rules
- May have served several **CUSTOMER**s, but not at the same time
- May never serve a **CUSTOMER** (e.g., may leave the company before serving a customer)
- Must have worked in one or more **OUTLET**s (may be transferred or may work part-time in several outlets)

Data Attributes
- salesperson name
- salesperson address
- salesperson phone # (mv)
- salesperson fax #
- salesperson email address (mv)

Unique Identifier
Salesperson-ID

Fig. 51: Object with Business Rules

And how do we go about asking the 'BRT Questions' of all the Objects that are part of a business process, so we can find all the rules?

Immediately upon completing a **Business Process Diagram** we start asking the 'BRT Questions' of our clients. As a result, we gain an understanding of the business rules in a specific context (a process) right away, which enables us to progressively understand better each answer we get from our clients. This approach also enables us to learn incrementally, which means that we don't have to start the project with a whole lot of knowledge.

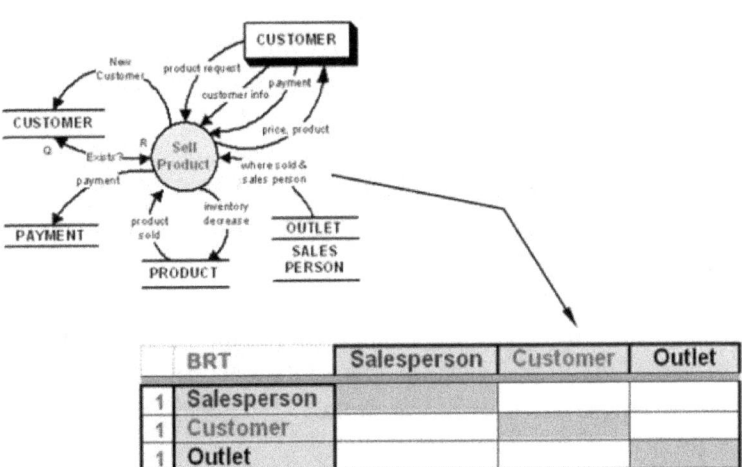

Fig. 52: Business Rules Table (BRT) – "Sell Product"

3.2 It's All About Asking Questions

It's important to recognize that analysis is all about asking questions … and thus finding the answers. The ability to do this quickly, without spinning wheels, is a function of asking the right questions, in context, the very first time. It's not about getting the answers from ourselves (and out of our own head) based on our hypothetical understanding of the client's business system, without ever talking to the client and subject-matter experts. It's about getting down with the clients and SMEs, and asking them all the relevant questions that have to be asked. And, it's about doing it quickly and effectively.

Sadly, many analysts – experienced ones and brand new ones – think it takes too much time to ask all the required questions of clients and SMEs. So they don't. The interesting thing about all the precise questions that come out of the individual **Business Rules Table**s is that … they actually help us get the work done faster than by not asking the questions. The questions identified by the individual **Business Rules Table**s focus on nothing but the rules of behavior between one group of data and another (i.e., Objects), in a context where these data come together. It doesn't get any tighter or more concise than that.

How many times has your client gone off on a tangent that appear to have little to do with the objectives of the project? How many times has your team experienced loss of focus in meetings or client-interactive sessions? How often have we heard the refrain, *"my client doesn't know what they want"*? All of these challenges can be attributed to meetings without a way of keeping everyone in focus and on target. And all of these challenges take time, time, time. It is simply faster and much more effective to go directly to the questions to be asked, ask them, and get immediate answers in variations of "yes", "no", "maybe" or "sometimes" – all of which can be decoded. Even though there may be scores of questions to ask our clients, it's a whole lot faster and better to know exactly what the questions are than to have to meander through the business analysis without focus. The other benefit is that you know when the entire job is done. It's not a guess. You know.

So, how fast can it get? Well, let's remember that any charlatan can finish faster than you simply by <u>not</u> doing some of the work required. But to know that the work is absolutely complete <u>*and*</u> it was finished fast, that's another matter. And that truly is "agile". I will give you a metric later in the book when we discuss how long it takes to complete a *discovery session* and the ensuing work, so we can have a measurable definition of "fast".

I mentioned earlier that at their core, most systems do just one thing: They keep track of stuff, so we can find the "stuff" later – or use it to make new "stuff". Therefore, based on the principle of finding the answer first and then discovering the question, it is the business analyst's job to discover what the client needs **to find**, and under what circumstances. By finding the circumstances (the *business events*) we can identify what it is we need to know, and therefore identify what we need to record or remember.

So what does all of this accomplish? By asking the questions generated by Object relationships in the BRT, it enables the following:

- It enables us to quickly find the specific business rules that determine required and disallowed behavior in a specific context.

- It enables us to find *business events* that had not yet been mentioned by the clients, and have not yet been discovered.

- It enables us to find Objects and data attributes that we need which have not yet been discovered.

- Based on discovering new *business events* (via the 4th 'BRT Question'), we may discover new Objects not previously defined; therefore, we will discover new data attributes and new business rules too.

- It enables us to eliminate scope creep due to errors of omission – things we didn't know to ask about, or our clients didn't think to tell us about.

The rules that come from the 'BRT Questions'– always in the singular context of a specific *business event* – are a different way of prescribing the behavior of the system, from an exclusive business context.

This means that the **Business Process Diagrams** (and accompanying text), along with Object definitions and the rules derived from the 'BRT Questions' *eliminate the need for other behavior models at the business specification level*. That reduces the amount of work needed considerably, while no facts or business requirements are missed. This is, at least in my definition of the universe, truly agile. (Yes, I will discuss how long this takes later.)

Also, all of the business rules that come from the 'BRT Questions' lead directly to test cases.

Each business rule is a clear and brief contextual specification of required (or disallowed) behavior. A test case of functionality can be easily built around each of these business rule statement. Since this is done up-front as part of the business discovery, it eliminates the need to spend an lot of time figuring out business functionality later; thus, more time is saved, and "agile" business analysis takes on more meaning.

3.3 You'll Need Clear Business Rules

By asking the 'BRT Questions' we can easily generate all the business rules needed for the project and the affected business areas, with each rule stated in a specific context. Each of the business rules is constructed from the responses we get after asking the 'BRT Questions', and all rules are written in plain language. Each rule is attributed and documented under the anchor Object that forms part of the 'BRT Question'. An example of how rules are attributed to an Object (**SALESPERSON**) is illustrated in Fig. 54, based on the limited **Business Rules Table** (Fig. 53).

	BRT	Salesperson	Customer	Outlet
1	Salesperson		N, 0	1, N
1	Customer			
1	Outlet			

Fig. 53: Business Rules Table (BRT) – Salesperson Relationships

Fig. 54: Object with Business Rules

Business rules should be written as simple, single-subject declarative statements. This helps the reader understand exactly what we mean when we document the rules, and we never have to rely on someone else's comprehension of the language or their intuitive understanding.

The 'BRT Questions' we ask our clients solicit clear, unambiguous answers, which can only be *"yes," "no"* or *"sometimes"* and *"maybe"* (which we'll get to soon). We use shorthand (e.g., 0, 1, or N) to note our clients' answers, and we call this shorthand **multiplicity** or **cardinality** or, *the ratio of occurrences between the anchor Object and its intersecting Objects.* The ratio of occurrences that's entered in the cell that joins two Objects indicates how we should write the business rules.

For example:

- If there is a **1** only we write, "**must be only one {OBJECT}**" as the business rule statement.

- If there is a value of **1, N** only we write, "**must be one or more {OBJECTs}**" as the business rule statement.

- If there is a value of **N** only we write, "**must be several {OBJECTs}**" as the business rule statement.

- If there is a value of **1, N, 0** we write, "**must be one or more {OBJECTs} ... unless there are none**"; or we can write "**may be several {OBJECTs} ... unless there are none**" as the business rule statement. We can also write two rules for the **1, N, 0** relationship, such as "**may be one or more {OBJECTs}**" ..." followed by "**may never be an {OBJECT}...**".

- If there is a value of **N, 0** we write "**must be more than one {OBJECT} ... unless there are none**"; or we can write "**must be several {OBJECTs} ... unless there are none**" as the business rule statement.

- If there is a **0** value, we write "**will never have an {OBJECT}...**" as a separate business rule statement.

In all of the above I have used the relationship verb "to be" or "to have" to join the anchor and intersecting Objects. Below, there are examples of these rules, written in plain language, with verb constructs other than the generic "to be".

- If here is a **1** only we can write, under the **CUSTOMER** Object, "**must receive only one PAYMENT**" as the business rule statement.

BRT		Customer	Payment
1	**Customer**		1
1	Payment		

Fig. 55: BRT Object with "1" entry

- If there is a value of **1, N** we can write, under the **CUSTOMER** Object, "**must receive one or more PAYMENTs**" as the business rule statement.

BRT		Customer	Payment
1	**Customer**		1, N
1	Payment		

Fig. 56: BRT Object with "1, N" entry

- If there is a value of **N** only we can write, under the **CUSTOMER** Object, "**must receive several PAYMENTs**" as the business rule statement.

	BRT	Customer	Payment
1	**Customer**		N
1	Payment		

Fig. 57: BRT Object with "N" entry

- If there is a value of **1, N, 0** we can write, "**must receive one or more PAYMENTs ... unless there are none**"; or we can write "**may receive several PAYMENTs ... unless there are none**" as the business rule statement. We can also write two rules for the **1, N, 0** relationship, such as "**may receive one or more PAYMENTs**" ..." followed by "**may never receive a PAYMENT...**".

	BRT	Customer	Payment
1	**Customer**		1. N. 0
1	Payment		

Fig. 58: BRT Object with "1,N,0" entry

- If there is a value of **N, 0** we can write "**must receive more than one PAYMENT ... unless there are none**"; or we can write "**must receive several PAYMENTs ... unless there are none**" as the business rule statement.

	BRT	Customer	Payment
1	**Customer**		N. 0
1	Payment		

Fig. 59: BRT Object with "N,0" entry

- If there is a **0** value only, we write "**<u>will</u> never receive a <u>PAYMENT</u>...**" as a separate business rule statement.

BRT		Customer	Payment
1	**Customer**		0
1	Payment		

Fig. 60: BRT Object with "0" entry

As you can imagine, it's very important to be precise (i.e., *exact, as in measurement or amount*) and concise (i.e., *expressing much in few words*) when writing the business rules. The shorthand notation of 1, N and 0 tells us just about everything, but it doesn't put the relationship in the context of a chosen verb construct. Therefore, we write out the rule in plain language, joining the two related Objects in a relationship described by the chosen verb. While the simple cardinality of 1, N and 0 may be enough for database designers, the business folks need to see the rule written out clearly, in plain business language.

3.4 Complementary Business Events

The *business event* is the foundation for all business processes. In other words, if there is no situation or circumstance to deal with (which is how we define a *business event*) then there is no need for a process. Finding *business event*, then, is the most important job of all.

Most *business events* have complementary *business events* – counterparts. Some *business events* must have opposite ends, or the project would not be complete in its logical coverage. Finding these is not a strange journey to a mysterious land. All we have to do is to identify the <u>complementary</u>, <u>opposite</u>, <u>predecessor</u> or subsequent *business event* and then ask the client if it is a *situation* or *circumstance* that they want to keep track of. A couple of examples of questions you might want to ask to determine *business events* that fall into these categories follow.

- You have identified the *business event* "**The Customer Buys a Product**" as being within the scope of your project. Does the complementary *business event* "**The Customer Returns a Product**" also fall inside the scope of the project? Are these returns something you want to keep track of?

- "**It is Time to Order a Product from a Supplier**" has been identified as a *business event* inside your project's scope. Does the subsequent *business event* "**The Product Arrives from the Supplier**" also belong to the project? Do you want to keep track of products that arrive from suppliers?

- "**A Vendor Applies for Approval to be a Recognized Vendor**" has been identified as a *business event* inside your project's scope. Do the related *business events* "**The Vendor is Suspended**" and "**The Vendor Ceases Operation**" also belong to the project? Do you want to keep track of suspended vendors or vendors that cease operations?

As we discussed earlier, the "keep track of" question is far better to use than asking if something is inside a project's scope. Asking about scope is a bit abstract for most people (notice how they scrunch their eyebrows as they think about this), whereas asking "do you want to keep track of <xyz>" becomes a whole lot easier to deal with.

Finding these complementary or related *business events* is making sure we ask the client all the follow-on questions that come as a result of discovering other *business events*. Finding the opposite end of a *business event* is making sure nothing is left unasked. Finding these complementary *business events* is establishing the limits to the project by stepping out to its perimeter and beyond and then determining where the scope line comes to rest. Scope creep will always be a challenge unless there is some way to determine the limits to the project. You can use the **Business Rules Table** and the 'BRT Questions' to determine what's in and what's out, but you also need to look for the complementary *business events* that make up the whole.

3.5 What Makes a Good Question?

Open-ended questions are good for stimulating discussion but not so good for getting clear and specific answers. Therefore, we rarely ask open-ended questions like, *"what do we need to know about customers?"* Not only will an answer take a long time, but we have no reasonable hope of achieving specific answers with such a question. This kind of question, while it might create interesting discussion, really just transfers the responsibility for analysis from the business analyst to the client or subject-matter expert. Most (but not all) open-ended questions do not lend anything of value to "agile" business analysis. Instead, we have to ask simple and closed-ended questions about the data (Objects) that's needed to support a process. We do this with closed-ended questions through the **Business Rules Table** and the 'BRT Questions', which tends to encourage direct and unusually concise answers. They cause answers such as *"yes," "no"* and *"no, that's not what I mean."*

While I strongly support the idea of open-ended questions to stimulate discussion and brainstorming – which is sometimes very necessary – I equally strongly discourage this approach if the objective is to get concise answers to specific questions quickly. The idea of "agile" business analysis also means getting clear and concise answers to questions quickly. Since the 'BRT Questions' have a specific syntax, they are designed to elicit exact answers rapidly.

The idea of using closed-ended questions based on a specific predefined syntax also removes business system analysis from the realm of 'art', as so many have called it (an elitist idea, if I ever heard one). The 'art', as I understand it, has always been finding the questions to ask. And whoever was good at finding better questions – and therefore got better and faster answers – was considered to be the best and most experienced analyst. The **Business Rules Table** and the 'BRT Questions' enable all of us to become artists.

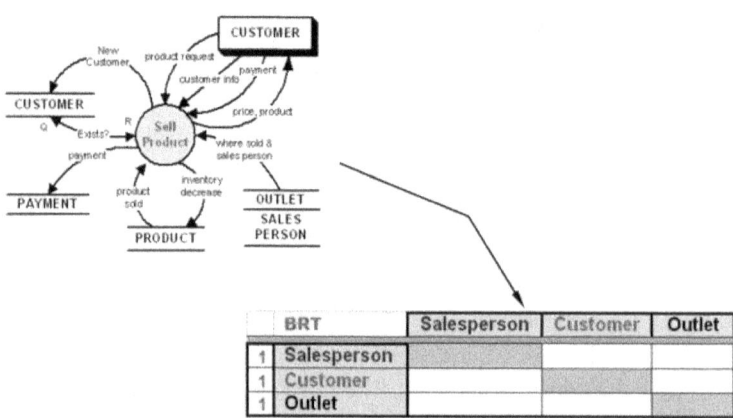

Fig. 61: Business Rules Table (BRT) – Questions about Objects specific to a Process

3.6 Sometimes the Answer is "It depends"

Sometimes, when we ask questions of clients or SMEs we get answers like *"well, it depends…"* or *"maybe"* or *"sometimes"*. While these answers are often seen as frustratingly vague or evasive, and may even appear defensive, it's really quite the opposite.

Sometimes, in real life, the answer is … *"it depends"*. This is simply a conditional response; that is, under one circumstance the answer is *"no"*, while under another circumstance the answer is *"yes"*. You will recall that a *business event* is a "condition or circumstance …." One of the two circumstances suggested by an 'it depends' type of answer is most likely a *business event* that you have already found, while the other one has not yet been discovered and added to your **Project Business Event List**. This kind of answer, then, is an opportunity to find a new *business event* that's not so obvious. To find it, we ask the client, *"Can you give me a couple of the situations or circumstances you're thinking about?"* Undoubtedly, they will, and you will then discover one or more new *business events* that weren't considered before. Add the new *business events* to your **Project Business Event List (Parking Lot)**, and then –working with your project subject-matter experts – develop the new **Business Process Diagrams** that support those *business events*.

3.7 How to Use Verbs in the 'BRT Questions'

So far, I have said very little about how to select the verb construct to bind the two Objects in the 'BRT Question' together so you can have a context for the question. Let me remind you of how the 'BRT Questions' are structured:

QUESTION # 1:

Structure: "Could the {anchor OBJECT} {relationship context verb} just one {intersecting OBJECT}?"

Or, in plain English:

"Could the SALESPERSON serve just one CUSTOMER?" (Answer: *"Yes."*)

QUESTION # 2:

Structure: "Could the {anchor OBJECT} {relationship context verb} several {intersecting OBJECTs}?"

Or, in plain English:

"Could the SALESPERSON serve several CUSTOMERs?" (Answer: *"Yes."*)

QUESTION # 3:

Structure: "Might the {anchor OBJECT} never {relationship context verb} any {intersecting OBJECTs} at all?"

Or, in plain English:

"Might the SALESPERSON never serve any CUSTOMERs at all?" (Answer: *"Yes."*)

QUESTION # 4: "Under what circumstances might that be true?" (Answer: *"They leave the company before they serve their first customer."*)

All of these questions are based on the **Business Rules Table** in Fig. 62, with the answers written as 1, N, 0 under <u>CUSTOMER</u> and across from <u>SALESPERSON</u>.

BRT		Customer
1	**Salesperson**	1, N, 0
1	Customer	

Fig. 62: Partial Business Rules Table (BRT) –
Salesperson : Customer

So, how did we know to use the verb *'to serve'*? Lucky guess? How do we know what the verb construct should be for any 'BRT Question'?

The verb you choose to use is determined by the business process you are dealing with. For example, if the process you're working on has to do with the sale of products to customers, the **Business Process Diagram** (Fig. 63) will have a verb assigned to it that defines the process under which the data is related.

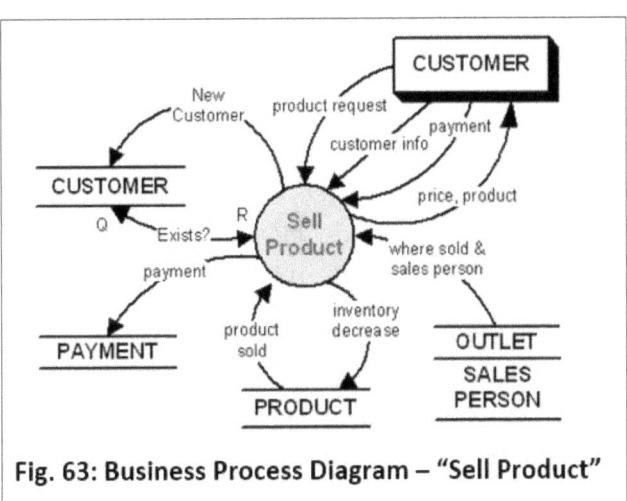

Fig. 63: Business Process Diagram – "Sell Product"

One way to find an appropriate verb to define the relationship between two Objects is to ask the clients or subject-matter experts who are present in your requirements *discovery* sessions. After all, they know their business.

However, if you do this I guarantee that you will get lots and lots of debate about what the right verb could be. If there are seven people in the room with you, you'll get eleven opinions on what's right and what's wrong. The reason for this is because you're asking them an open-ended question *("So, what verb might we use here?")*, which is designed for discussion rather than a direct answer. So, don't go there. You'll spin wheels 'til the cows come home.

It is far better that you select what you think is an appropriate verb (right or wrong) and go with that. The important point is that the verb you chose must be contextual – that is, in the context of the business process – and must make sense in your 'BRT Questions'. The chosen verb will not necessarily be the one you used in the **Business Process Diagram**, like "**Sell Product**" in the earlier process (Fig. 63). But your chosen verb will reflect the context of that process. In the example we used earlier, based on this process, we used the verb "to serve" since this worked better in constructing the 'BRT Questions'.

But what about those situations when you have no idea what the right verb might be? What then? Out of all your verb choices in the language, you clearly can't just make one up without it making some kind of sense. So, what to do?

The answer, as with all good things, is with Shakespeare. The Bard had many good things to say, and arguably his most famous of all was The Question; which is precisely what we are discussing now – the 'BRT Question'. My friend Shakespeare wrote, *"To be or not to be ... that is the question."*

To be.

But to use this effectively we have to start with the very first placeholder question. An example is below.

PLACEHOLDER QUESTION: **"For a single, specific SALESPERSON how many CUSTOMERs might there be?"** (Do not wait for an answer.)

We follow this immediately with the next three (and possibly four) 'BRT Questions'. However, to use the verb *'to be'* we have to slightly restructure the questions, as follows:

- 1ˢᵗ Question: **"Could there be just <u>one</u> CUSTOMER?"** (Answer: *"Yes."*)

- 2ⁿᵈ Question: **"Could there be <u>several</u> CUSTOMERs?"** (Answer: *"Yes."*)

- 3ʳᵈ Question: **"Might there never be <u>any</u> CUSTOMERs at all?"** (Answer: *"Yes."*)

- 4ᵗʰ Question: **"Under what circumstances might that be true?"** (Answer: *"The salesperson leaves the company before they serve their first customer."*)

	BRT	Customer
1	Salesperson	1, N, 0
1	Customer	

Fig. 64: Partial Business Rules Table –
Salesperson : Customer

To make the questions work, the subject (**SALESPERSON**) is now mentioned in the placeholder question only, and it is implied in the subsequent questions. But it works, even though it can sometimes be awkward. I certainly wouldn't want to see a **Business Requirements Document** with the verb *'to be'* documented throughout all the Objects in the project. However, the purpose of this Shakespearean tactic is not to find the final verb, but to find a way of starting so your business partners and subject-matter experts can move ahead quickly. If necessary, you can change the verb construct later. This approach works extremely well; and has kept many discovery sessions rolling along without those awkward discussions when everyone in the room is arguing about what the right verb might be.

3.8 Are Opposite Ends of the Business Rules Table the Same?

There is a commonly held misperception that opposite ends of intersecting Objects must be the same. This is incorrect. Let me explain.

In the **Business Rules Table** in Fig. 65, the relationship cell **SALESPERSON-CUSTOMER** contains **"NA"**, which means the client has decided that this relationship is 'not applicable' to their business requirements. There could be any number of reasons why they have no interest in this relationship. One possibility is that it's outside the scope of the project. In such a case, this relationship cell would produce no business rules that can contribute to the project.

BRT	Salesperson	Customer
1 Salesperson		NA
1 Customer	1, N, 0	

Fig. 65: Partial Business Rules Table – Salesperson : Customer

The opposite end of this relationship, **CUSTOMER-SALESPERSON**, contains **1, N, 0** which would produce a full set of rules, and may even identify a new *business event* in the reason for the "0" relationship.

BRT	Salesperson	Customer
1 Salesperson		NA
1 Customer	1, N, 0	

Fig. 66: Partial Business Rules Table – Salesperson : Customer

It is definitely not true that the relationship between two Objects must be the same from both directions. Neither is it true that a relationship between two Objects will be different in the opposite direction.

Part 4.
The Business Processes

The business processes are arguably the most important part of the business and system requirements to your business partners and subject-matter experts. They think in terms of *what the system should do*, while the analyst must think in terms of what information the system <u>must know about</u> and <u>have access to</u> so it can support the business. That means we really have to focus on the Objects and the business rules. The Objects define the data we have to keep track of, and the business rules define the circumstances under which required data must exist. Your clients and subject-matter experts, however, will naturally want to focus on the processes required by the system, and what those processes should do.

Before exploring business processes, we need to better understand the components that make up those processes, and we need to understand that a 'process model' can't stand on its own. The **Business Requirements Document** must consist of **all** required documentation, not just diagrams that describe the processes.

4.1 The Requirements Document

The **Business Requirements Document** is organized first by *business event* and secondly by Object, with each Object being defined only once.

You will recall that a *business event* is an essential <u>condition</u>, a <u>circumstance</u>, a <u>situation</u>, a <u>state</u> or an <u>external requirement</u> that the target business area must respond to or deal with in order to successfully support the organization's key business objectives, goals, or mission.

A *business event* also does not reflect **_how_** something is done; it represents **_what_** must be done without regard to a particular technology or a particular way of doing things.

You will recall that *business events* come in four flavors:

Situation Event – non-controlled
"The Customer Buys a Product"
"The Product Shipment Arrives from a Supplier"
"The Customer has Exceeded Their Credit Limit"

External Event – based on third party need
"The Government Requires Notification of
   Employee Earnings"
"The Customer Requests a Higher Credit Limit"

Temporal Event – based on time
"The Customer's Credit Card Expires"
"It is Time to Pay the Supplier"
"It is Time to Increase the Customer's Credit Limit"

Internal Event – based on a decision
"The Company Decides to Cancel the Customer's
   Credit Card"
"The Company Decides to Issue a Loan to the
   Customer"

Also, *business events* never start with a verb. That's because a *business event* is not a process. A *business event* is a condition, circumstance, state or external requirement that must be supported by a process. The process that supports a *business event* is illustrated by, preferably, a **Business Process Diagram**, which is similar to (looks like) but not the same as a data flow diagram. However, the **Business Process Diagram** limits itself to one process only, rather than several. This, too, goes to the idea that we should "partition the effort to minimize complexity" and therefore be more "agile" in approaching business requirements.

Some of my colleagues insist that both data models and process models are necessary for a complete requirements specification. I see it differently. That's very old-school, and takes a lot of unnecessary time. Data models represent essentially a database view. Our business partners and clients really have no interest in the database view. Their primary interest is in business functionality, and appropriate deployment of technology to support their business needs. However, in addition to business behavioral rules, the accesses to data that are required by the target business area are described in the **Business Rules Tables** that support each process. While this is mostly transparent to your business partners, database analysts and designers should recognize **Business Rules Tables** as prescriptions for database access based on the requirements of the business.

The Business Requirements Document

Project Business Event List

A list of project *business events*, including business area ownership and involvement, and requirement priority.

For each Event (*n* occurrences)

- A **Business Process Diagram** that supports the *business event*.
- A task-based narrative for the Business process.
- References or links to Object definitions.
- A list of Business Areas affected by the Business process
- A Business Rules Table for Objects supporting the business process.
- Any Implementation (design solution) considerations.

For each Object (*n* occurrences)

- Definition of the Object.
- Business Rules for the Object.
- Data attributes for the Object.
- Primary (unique) identifier.

The Business Rules Table (BRT)

- Matrix of intersecting Objects.
- Cardinality (0,1,N) for each Object.

BRT		customer	product	payment
1	customer		1,N,0	1,N,0
1	product	1,N,0		1,N,0
1	payment	1	1,N	

Fig. 67: Example of a Business Rules Table (BRT)

Business Process Diagram symbols

The Business Process Diagram.

The **Business Process Diagram** illustrates the required tasks and planned responses of the target business area to a specific *business event*. Each **Business Process Diagram** must have a written narrative to describe the process. This narrative supports the diagram so readers of the documentation can understand the business requirements. The diagram must have definitions of all the participating Objects, their data attributes, and business rules. A single **Business Process Diagram** can support more than one *business event*.

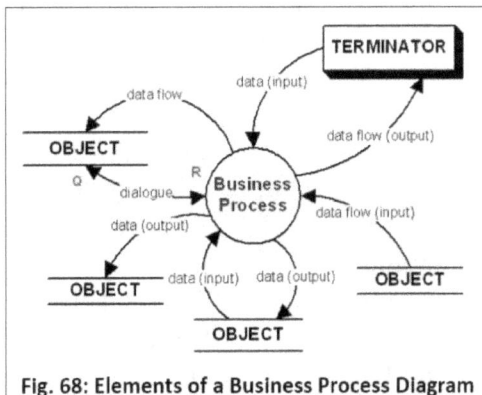

Fig. 68: Elements of a Business Process Diagram

Fig. 68 is an illustration of the components of a **Business Process Diagram**, and Fig. 69 is a diagram specific to the business event "The Customer Buys a Product".

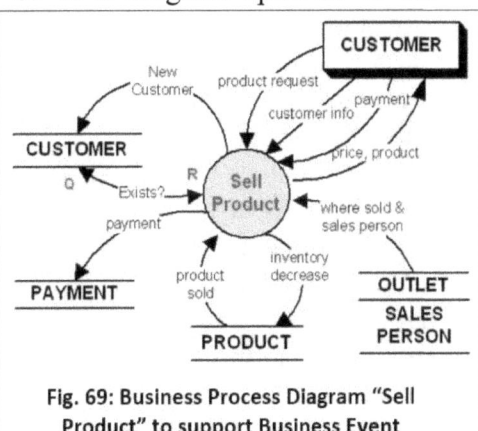

Fig. 69: Business Process Diagram "Sell Product" to support Business Event "Customer Buys a Product"

While a picture is worth a thousand words, this diagram is not sufficient to describe business requirements: It needs a brief narrative, Object definitions, data attributes and business rules before it is complete.

The Terminator.

A Terminator is a source of information or destination for information from a process. A Terminator, which may be inside or outside your organization, is not directly under the control of the business process which receives it or sends information to it. A Terminator has its own set of processes and data, but these are outside the domain of the process that interfaces with it. *Use Case* practitioners might call a Terminator an "Actor", but that's only part of the story. It is definitely not a **Primary Actor** (one who does something in the system, since that implies a "how" or a technology, since there are three kinds of technologies: Software, hardware and peopleware). However, a Terminator can be either or both a **Secondary Actor** (provides a service or data) and an **Offstage Actor** (has an interest in the system, and receives data). A Terminator is simply a source or a destination of information. Some, but not all Terminators are also Objects in our business processes; but only if we need to remember something about the Terminator, or need to look it up (among several) so information can be sent to it.

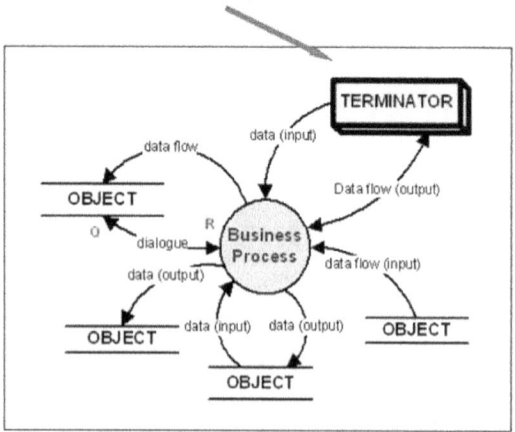

Fig. 70: Business Process Diagram - The "Terminator"

The Object.

An Object is a repository of data shown in **Business Process Diagrams**.

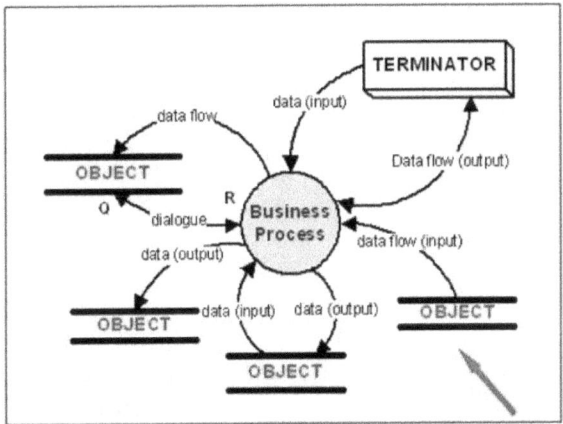

Fig. 71: Business Process Diagram - The "Object"

- An Object is a repository of logically grouped non-redundant data.

- An Object in a **Business Process Diagram** contains all the data items attributed to the Object, in accordance with **The 5 Business Data Rules**.

- An Object in a **Business Process Diagram** contains all the business rules attributed to it from the **Business Rules Table** specific to that **Business Process Diagram** (see Part 3: The Business Rules Table).

The Process Narrative.

A task-based process narrative must be written for each **Business Process Diagram** in plain language. It must specify clearly what is to be done with each data flow and describes the planned response to support the business process. It can be written in either of two styles: Point form or structured narrative.

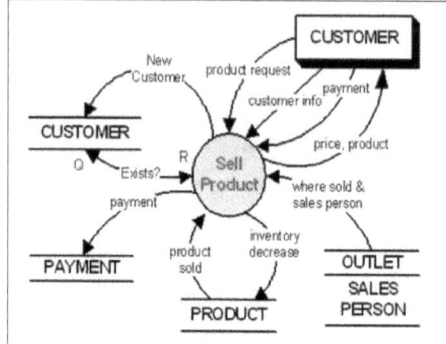

Fig. 72: Business Process Diagram – with 2 Narrative Styles

Point Form Style

For each request for a product from the customer:

● Find out if the **CUSTOMER** exists in our system.
● Find the **PRODUCT** sold.
● If it is available, give it to the **CUSTOMER** with the price.
● Accept the **PAYMENT** from the **CUSTOMER**.
● Remember the **PAYMENT**.
● Remember the **SALESPERSON** who served the **CUSTOMER**, and in which **OUTLET**.
● Reduce inventory by the quantity of **PRODUCT** sold.
● If it is a new **CUSTOMER**, get the **CUSTOMER** information from the customer.
● Remember the new **CUSTOMER** information.

Fig. 73: Task-based Narrative –
Point-form Style

Structured Narrative Style

For each request for a product from the customer, find the **PRODUCT**. If it is available give it to the **CUSTOMER** with the cost. Accept the **PAYMENT** from the **CUSTOMER**. Remember the **PAYMENT** and the sales transaction, including the **SALESPERSON** who served the **CUSTOMER**, and in which **OUTLET**. Reduce inventory by the quantity of the **PRODUCT** sold. If it is a new customer, remember the **CUSTOMER**.

Fig. 74: Task-based Narrative –
Structured Style

The Data flow.

A *data flow* represents the directional movement of information between a process and an Object or Terminator. A data flow must always be labeled for its contents when the data flow is between a process and a Terminator. However, it does not have to be labeled if it is between the process and an Object. This is because an Object is about one thing, and one thing only. While a data flow may only contain some of the data in an Object, the Object itself is not mystery data.

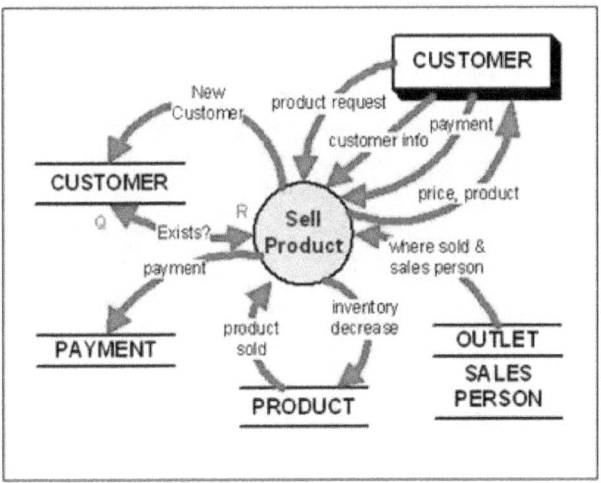

**Fig. 75: Business Process Diagram –
Illustrating Data Flows (Bold Lines)**

An Object is *something* specific. It is helpful, however, to always label a data flow since this makes it clear what is "riding" the data flow. You don't have to use data item names. Label it any way you like, as long as the label communicates effectively what the data flow is all about. This means the reader has to understand it, not just the writer.

The Dialogue Data flow.

A dialogue data flow is a data flow with arrows at each end showing the "dialogue" between a process and (a) an Object that contains data, or (b) a Terminator. For example, to query the **CUSTOMER** Object we can put the query "*exists*?" on the data flow, and a "**Q**" (for query) and "**R**" (for response) on each end of the data flow to illustrate that there is a dialogue.

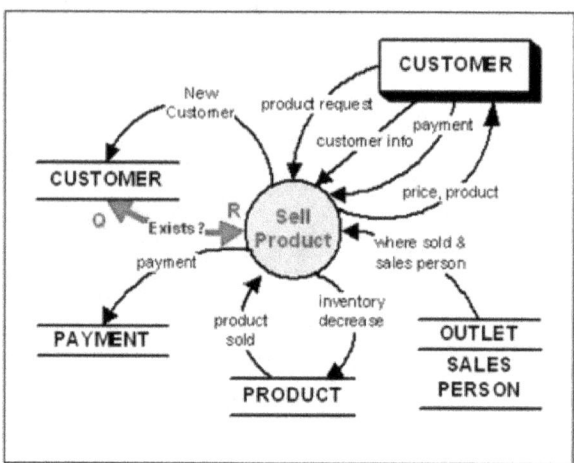

Fig. 76: Business Process Diagram –
Illustrating a Dialogue (Bold Lines)

Strict use of data item names on a data flow is not required. You can put anything you like on the data flow if it helps you to communicate better. If an Object is well named and properly attributed with data, without redundancy, then it will not be a mystery to know what data the Object consists of. One thing for sure: An Object will not be a variety-show data store containing all kinds of information about all kinds of things. Because Objects are limited in content it enables you to use data flows better, even putting verbs on them.

Stacked Objects.

Diagrams can sometimes get pretty busy, especially if there are a lot of participating Objects. So, we sometimes stack Objects to conserve space, as you see in Fig. 77. But we can't stack all the Objects, making one big stack, which would not be helpful in understanding the diagram. Objects should only be stacked if they are related to the subject of the data flows – such as the example in Fig. 77.

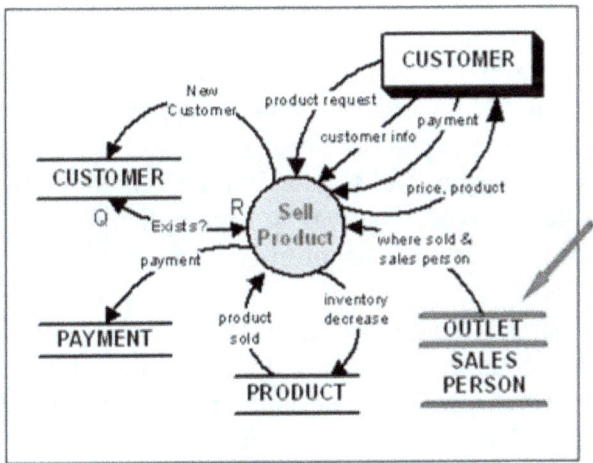

**Fig. 77: Business Process Diagram –
Illustrating related Stacked Objects**

4.2 A Business Requirements Example

The example we have selected to go through in considerable detail is a (partial) personal *accounts payable* system. We all have one of these for our personal expenses. It might be great software app, or it might be really simple. Since it is intended as an example of how to go through the steps to create a business requirements specification, we are not going to go down every possible road in terms of variable answers to questions or other such considerations. It's an example, and much in real life can be different.

Find Some Business Events First

The first step is to produce a short (or long) list of *business events* – conditions, circumstances, situations and other external requirements – that the target business area must include in its scope. One of the first objectives is to get together with all the senior project people – the sponsors, the key stakeholders, the business and subject-matter experts – and outline how the work will progress, what it will look like and how long it will take. In other words, to manage expectations. Part of managing expectations is to get a real handle on the project's scope, and to have the agreement of the key people involved. The way to accomplish this, we have found, is to create a list of in-scope *business events*.

We can get initial *business events* from the business and subject-matter experts by leading an interactive session that searches out the desired *business events* for the project. This presumes that your business experts know their business and they have a pretty good idea of what they need to support their business needs – not the technology application, but the business functionality. (Your clients do know their business. With well-structured and focused questions, we will always get precise answers from them.)

You certainly don't have to find all the *business events* that might make up your project. That would be difficult, at best. All you need is a few entries on a short list to get you started. If you have just a few *business events*, then you will be able to find all the others through answers to your 'BRT Questions', and specifically the fourth question – "under what circumstances would that be true?"

In this example we'll limit ourselves to starting with just two *business events*. However, we expect to find other *business events* through the 'BRT Questions', and if we do (and they are in scope) we'll add them to our **Project Business Event List (Parking Lot)** so we can work on them later.

The **Project Business Event List** is the list of *business* *events* we develop during the detailed discovery sessions with subject-matter experts. Several new *business events* are usually discovered during client-interactive discovery sessions; some that were not even thought to be part of the project. These are usually found in answers to the fourth 'BRT Question', although some are also found when the Object and Data Inclusion and Exclusion Questions are asked. As new in-scope *business events* are discovered, they are added to the **Project Business Event List (Parking Lot)**, and we can return to them when it's time to do so. In this way, progress is also very visible to clients, and there is no *"trust me, we'll deal with it later"*.

This book, the one you're reading now, is about business process modeling and not about the *discovery sessions* with clients and subject-matter experts. But you can find out everything you need to know about discovery sessions in my book about the subject.

Just search Amazon for my name or the title, and you'll find it. It's available as a hardcopy or digital from Kindle.

In our partial (personal) accounts receivable example, we'll work through the two basic business events we've identified.

> **Project Business Event List**
> - A Bill Arrives from a Supplier
> - It is Time to Pay a Supplier

Fig. 78: Initial Project Event List

The first *business event* is, "**A Bill Arrives from a Supplier**".

Business Process Diagrams

The first question we ask is, *"How do I know that … (insert event statement here).* For example, for our *business event* "**A Bill Arrives from a Supplier**" the question would be *"How do I know that a bill arrives from a supplier?"*

In this case the answer could be, *"We know the bill arrived from the supplier because we received it in the mail."*

The "mail" can, of course, mean many things. It could mean the bill arrived in the mailbox attached to your house or apartment, or it could be the mailbox in your computer. If we specify either of these "physical" options at this stage in the project, then we are biasing the solution design, or at the very least we are limiting ourselves to our current way of thinking. This would make it all the more difficult to discover re-engineering opportunities when we look at the potential design solutions later.

Instead, we look for the basic concept behind "mail" and the *net flow of data*.

What this means is … we look for the source of the data, rather than the physical handler such as an email system or postal delivery. In our earlier definition of a Terminator we said, *"It is a source of input…"* from outside the system. In this example we get the bill from a supplier. We illustrate this by using **Business Process Diagram** symbols, showing the process as a bubble, and the data we received from the supplier as a data flow with an arrow from the supplier as input to the process in our system.

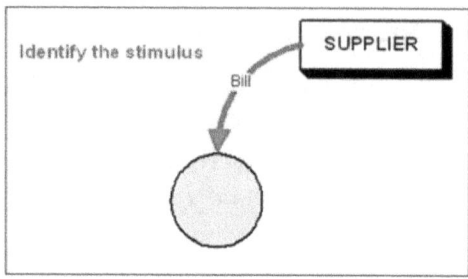

Fig. 79: Business Process "stimulus"

The second question is, *"What are we going to do about it?"* In our accounts payable example, it means we have to determine what we're going to do with the bill after we receive it. While the immediate response might simply be, *"pay it,"* that's covered by our second *business event*, **"It is Time to Pay a Supplier"**.

We must always stay focused on the current *business event* to the exclusion of all others. In other words, **Business Process Diagrams** are joined by data, through Objects, and never through the flow of data. By trying to join various processes by way of data flows, rather than data items that make up Objects, we would end up with meta-*business events* that include everything, such as **"A Bill Arrives from a Supplier"** and **"It is Time to Pay a Supplier"**. If you end up doing a whole lot of things that are lumped together this way, you're probably violating our first analysis principle of "partition the effort to minimize complexity".)

Returning to what we're going to do with the bill we receive from the supplier (such as a phone bill), the question was *"What are we going to do about it?"* Our project subject-matter expert has informed us, *"We only accept bills from recognized and approved suppliers."*

With that information, we can add two data flows to our **Business Process Diagram**, as shown in Fig. 80. Each data flow represents a task.

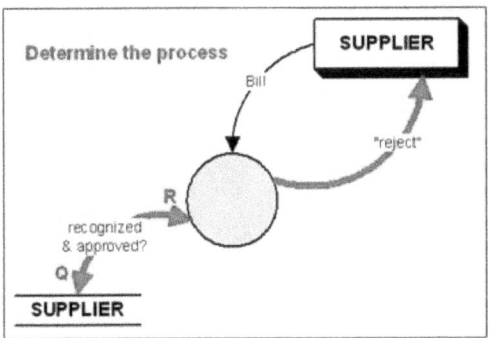

Fig. 80: Business Process "tasks"

In a real business system we would, of course, check the bill against a purchase order to determine its legitimacy. However, our example (minimized to reduce complexity) is a personal accounts payable system.

The last question to our subject-matter expert (SME) is, *"What do we need to record or remember about this process?"* In our example this means – now that we have received a bill and checked that it's from a recognized supplier – that we want to record the bill received from the supplier. We can draw this as illustrated in Fig. 81.

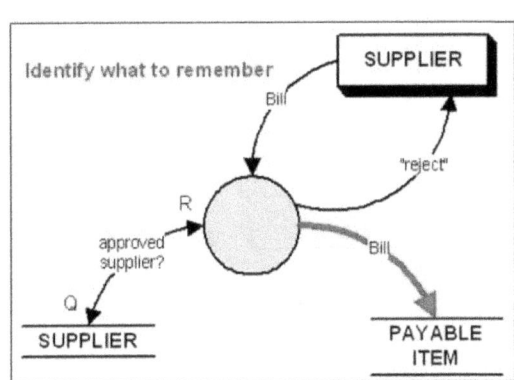

Fig. 81: Business Process "remembering data"

Before we go on to the next part, let's review how to determine the direction of the arrow on a diagram. Data flows (and their arrowheads) can only go in two directions – in or out of the process (the bubble). The data flow either goes out of the process or it comes into the process.

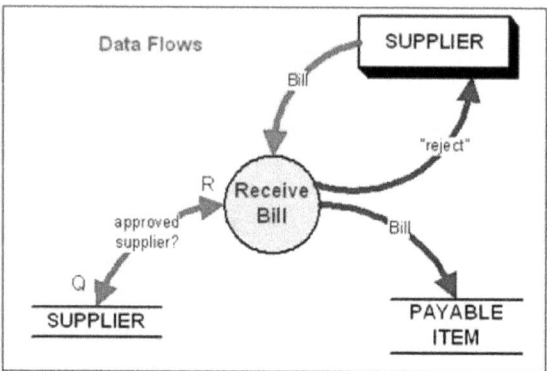

Fig. 82: Direction of Dataflows

When a data flow comes into the process (the bubble) it means we are retrieving data from an Object or we have received data from a Terminator.

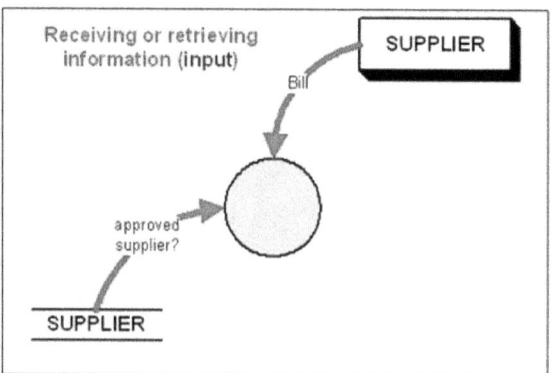

Fig. 83: Dataflows Coming into a Process

When a data flow goes out of a process, it means we are recording data in an Object or we are sending some form of data to a Terminator (i.e., to a destination outside the system or business unit's immediate processes).

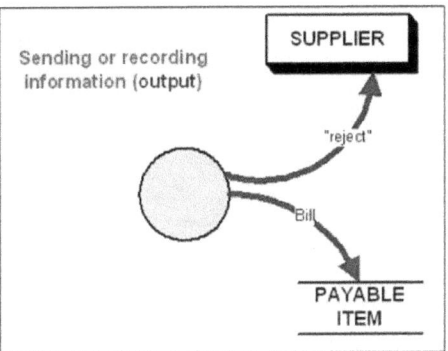

Fig. 84: Dataflows Going Out of a Process

When there is a dialogue data flow there are arrowheads on each end of the data flow. This represents two separate data flows – one to find the right record or data, and another to return the data – for the same subject data. By drawing a single data flow in this manner, we're just conserving space, and we're illustrating that something specific is directly related; i.e., two ends of the same thing. The **'Q'** represents "query", and the **'R'** represents "response". In the example in Fig. 85 we could read it as, *"Find the record of an approved supplier that matches the query. If the query finds that the supplier is on record and approved, tell me. If not, tell me that too."*

A dialogue data flow

R

approved
supplier?

Q

SUPPLIER

Fig. 85: Dialogue Dataflow

This now leaves us with a complete diagram for the *business event* "**A Bill Arrives from a Supplier**" (as shown in Fig. 86).

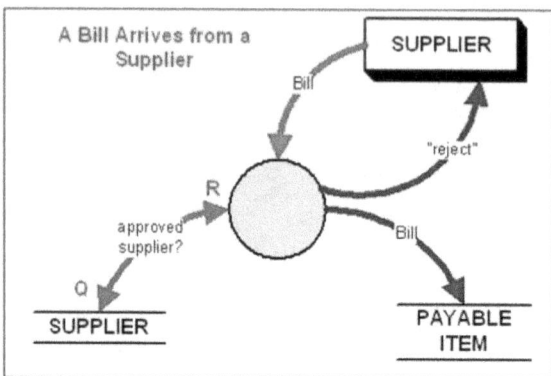

Fig. 86: Business Process Diagram to Support
Event "A Bill Arrives from a Supplier"

But lots of things haven't been done yet: We haven't given a name to the process and labeled it; nor have we written a narrative to describe it. We also haven't done any data discovery and attribution; and we haven't completed the **Business Rules Table** to find and document the business rules for Objects that support this particular circumstance, "**A Bill Arrives from a Supplier**".

Some of these things are done in parallel with the drawing of the **Business Process Diagram** to support a *business event*. This is particularly true for how we go about discovering Objects and how we go about attributing data items that we find. Creating the **Business Rules Table**, asking the 'BRT Questions', and generating the business rules is the very last thing that's done after the diagram has been completed, including writing the descriptive narrative and attributing data to the Objects.

You will recall that the very first question we asked our subject-matter experts was, *"How do I know that a bill arrives from a supplier?"* This resulted in finding the stimulus (bill arrives from supplier), which led to the partial diagram in Fig. 87.

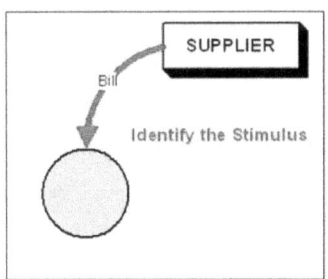

As the subject-matter experts answer the next question *("What are we going to do about it?")*, your SMEs could respond with an answer that might be at the highest level of abstraction or at the lowest level of detail. As an

Fig. 87: Business Process with "stimulus" Identified

analyst, it is your responsibility to decipher what they have said and to determine what's a data item and what's an Object.

Because we now have to find the data that supports the process, we usually supplement the original question with another: *"What do we need to know about or remember about this process?"* For each noun, you must determine if it consists of *two or more component parts*. If it does, it's a noun "with substance". That's an Object. If the noun does not consist of more than one data item, then it's just another data item for which you have to find a home.

Another way of initially identifying Objects that are needed to support a *business event* situation – and perhaps the best way to start – is to use the nouns you find in the *business event* statement itself.

For example, in the *business event* "**A Bill Arrives from a Supplier**" there are two nouns – <u>Bill</u> and <u>Supplier</u>. Are these nouns "of substance"? Can we imagine each of them consisting of two or more data items? Sure ... we can imagine the Object **BILL** consisting of data such as *due date* and *amount due*. The other Object, **SUPPLIER**, could include data items such as *supplier name*, *supplier address*, *contact name* and *phone number*.

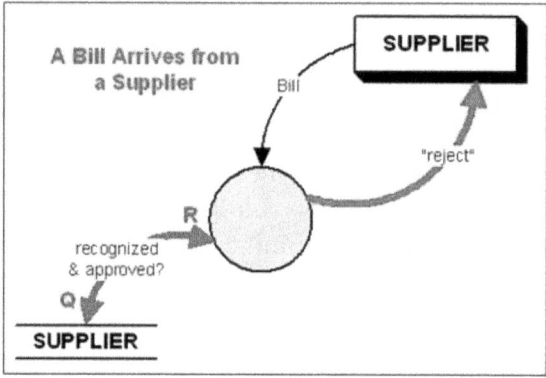

Fig. 88: Business Process with SUPPLIER Object

Since **SUPPLIER** is clearly an Object (see Fig. 89), then we must ask our subject-matter experts if they want a record of authorized suppliers. If the answer is *"yes,"* then we have an Object that we must document – and we can immediately attribute some of the data we uncovered.

SUPPLIER
- supplier name
- supplier address
- contact name
- phone #

Fig. 89: SUPPLIER Data Attributes

For **BILL,** we must ask our subject-matter experts if we want to remember (or record) the *due date* and *amount due*. If the answer is *"yes,"* then this is also an Object that we must include, and we can immediately attribute the data we uncovered.

PAYABLE ITEM
- Due date
- Amount due

Fig. 90: PAYABLE ITEM Data Attributes

These questions should stimulate other questions. We might even find the subject-matter experts want to call the bill a **PAYABLE ITEM**, and want to include some other data attributes (which we won't include here, so we can keep the example small).

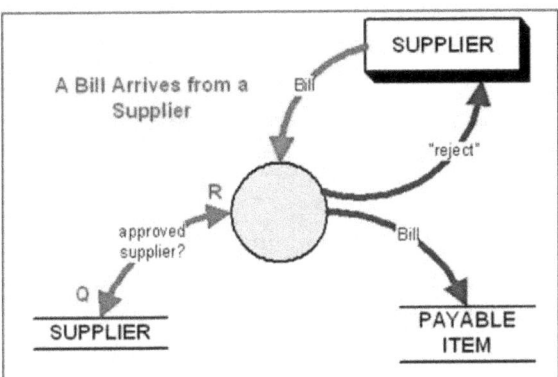

Fig. 91: Business Process with PAYABLE ITEM Object

Discussions with clients and subject-matter experts will tend to bring out the remaining Objects and the data that make up the Objects. In this particular example, there are no more Objects needed to support the *business event* "**A Bill Arrives from a Supplier**".

How do we know that we have put the data attributes with the right Objects? You will recall that Business Data Rule # 1 states, *"Attribute the data item to the Object it describes best, and to no other Object."* It appears that *due date* and *amount due* describe **PAYABLE ITEM** best, while *supplier name*, *supplier address*, *contact name* and *phone #* best describe **SUPPLIER**.

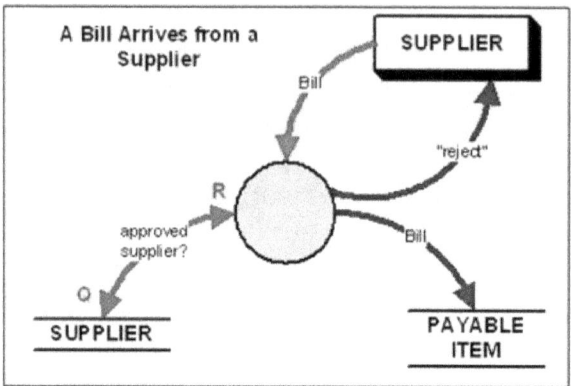

Fig. 92: Business Process supports the Event "A Bill Arrives from a Supplier"

The next step is to write a plain yet descriptive narrative. The narrative has to be clear, concise, unambiguous, in plain business language – and brief.

You will notice that at this time we have left the bubble that denotes the process unlabeled – blank and unnamed. That's intentional, and we're going to leave it unnamed until we have written the descriptive narrative necessary to support the diagram.

Our objective is to write a narrative that clearly explains the **Business Process Diagram** in as much detail as necessary, but no more. Our narrative must be in plain language – easily understood by our business partners – without any technobabble. We must stay away from writing great prose or even a novel. All of these are unnatural to our business partners. The end result must be a narrative that's easily understood by the business partners and the technical team.

So, where do you start? To help with the structure of the sentences, we have identified a few key words that will help you develop a usable narrative that's understandable to all. These five key words can be used to build just about any narrative:

1. "For each …"
2. "Periodically …"
3. "Determine …"
4. "Remember (or record) …"
5. "Find (or identify) …"

But how do we know exactly how many narrative statements are needed for any given business process? Is it simply stream-of-consciousness? Is it roaming around the china shop of words until we figure out what the text should be, based on brute thinking force? Does it require a major in English? Does it involve smoke and mirrors? Or will just plain magic do the trick?

Well, there is a way. Let me tell you about it.

We determine the narrative needed by identifying an implicit task for each data flow that comes into or goes out of the process. Visually, it looks like the illustration below (Fig. 93); although we don't draw those little nodes on our real diagrams, we just write the descriptive narratives.

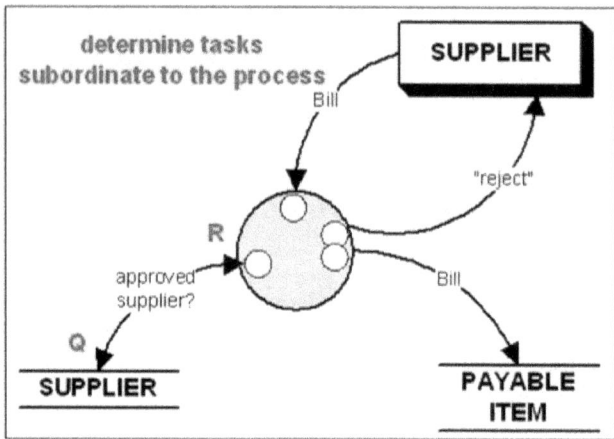

Fig. 93: Business Process with "task nodes" illustrated

Each of these nodes must have an explanatory narrative; or, better put, each node must be referenced in some way in the descriptive narrative that you write. You can use at least two different styles when producing your narrative, the Structured Narrative Style, or the Point Form Style. You can also develop your own style, as long as your narrative text refers to each of the data flows entering or leaving the process. You may have to add additional text to describe the transformation of data, such as calculations or other formulas.

For the **Business Process Diagram** below (which supports the *business event* "**A Bill Arrives from a Supplier**"), you could produce a narrative similar to either of the styles below the diagram.

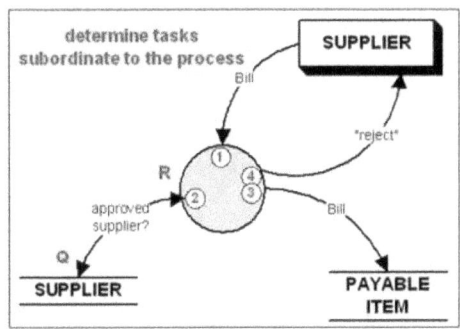

Fig. 94: Business Process with 2 types of Descriptive Narratives based on "task nodes"

Structured Narrative Style	Point Form Style
For each **bill** received, determine if it is from a recognized and approved **supplier**. If it is, remember it. If the **supplier** is not recognized, reject the **bill**.	1. Receive the **bill**. 2. Determine if it is from a recognized and approved **supplier**. 3. If it is, record it. 4. If the **supplier** is not recognized, reject the **bill**.

This form of *functional decomposition*, which is really process decomposition, is relatively straightforward. It enables you to quickly determine the tasks that make up a process.

Before we go on with our next *business event* in our accounts payable example, let's look at another example of process decomposition that enables us to easily write the narrative for the process.

For the diagram on the next page (Fig. 95), our objective is to pay the supplier for products received. Previous payments may already have been made (or not). After process decomposition to identify the subordinate tasks, we could have a task list, and narrative, as we see in the diagram.

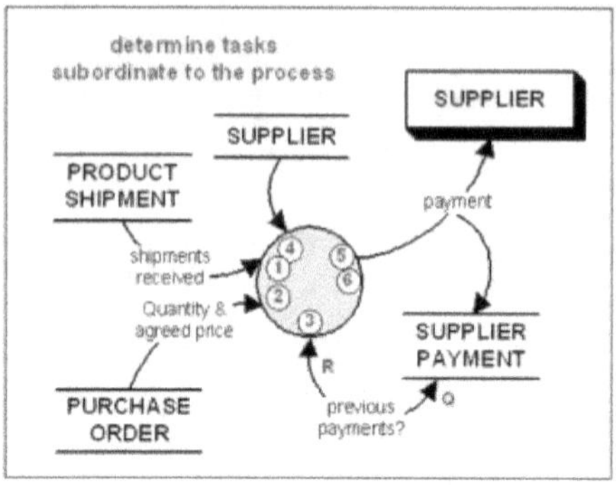

Point Form Style

1. Find **product shipments** not completely paid.
2. Determine the amount owed, based on the amount of **product** received and the agreed price.
3. Deduct any previous **payments** made against the same **purchase order**.
4. Find the **supplier**'s location and preferred method of payment.
5. Pay the **supplier**.
6. Record the **payment**.

Structured Narrative Style

Periodically, find those **shipments** received from **suppliers** that have not been completely paid. Determine the amount owed based on the amount of **product** received and the agreed price. Deduct any previous **payments** against the same **purchase order**. Pay the **supplier**, and remember the **payment**.

Fig. 95: Business Process with 2 types of Descriptive Narratives based on "task nodes"

Once again, you can write itemized tasks (Point Form Style), or you can write simple sentences (Structured Narrative Style), as shown in Fig, 95.

The *business event* in this case is "**It is Time to Pay a Supplier**". If a *business event* starts with "**It is Time to …**" we can often start the narrative with *"Periodically …"* The writing style you chose to use is the one you are most comfortable with.

The new element we introduced into this diagram, in Fig. 95, is what is called a *split* or *divergent data* flow. In the example diagram on the next page (Fig. 96), it means you are sending the payment to two places: the physical payment goes to the supplier (which could be a check or an electronic funds transfer); and the payment data is recorded so we can keep track of the supplier payment. While these two data flows that diverge represent the same thing (payment information), they will certainly be physically different in the implemented system.

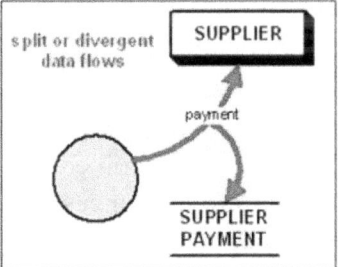

Fig. 96: Business Process with "Split" or "Divergent" Dataflow

In this example, relationships between Objects are absolutely necessary, because, as you'll recall from Business Data Rule # 1, an Object only contains data specific to that Object. If the Objects are not somehow joined, we would not be able to find what we need. For example, we need to find the **SUPPLIER** record for a specific **PURCHASE ORDER**.

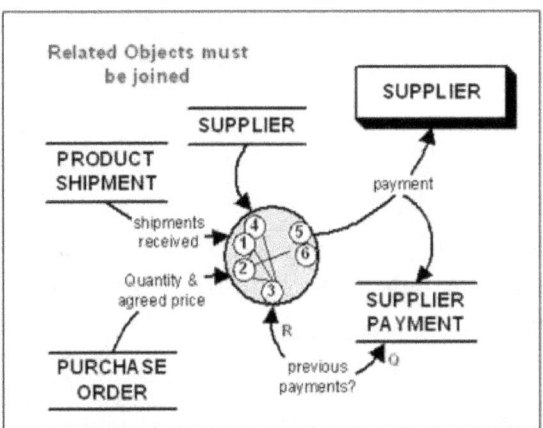

Fig. 97: Business Process – Objects Must be "joined" so they can be Relational

We also need to find all the **SUPPLIER PAYMENT** records for a specific **PURCHASE ORDER**. These relationships necessitate *foreign keys* to join the Objects that need to be joined. For us to create a business requirements specification that also consists of a prescription for the database design – but transparent to the client and the SMEs – we need to define which Objects must be joined to which other Objects under different circumstances (*business events*). We do this through the **Business Rules Table**.

We now have a complete diagram and narrative for the *business event* "**A Bill Arrives from a Supplier**". We have also identified the Objects and data items we need to support the process.

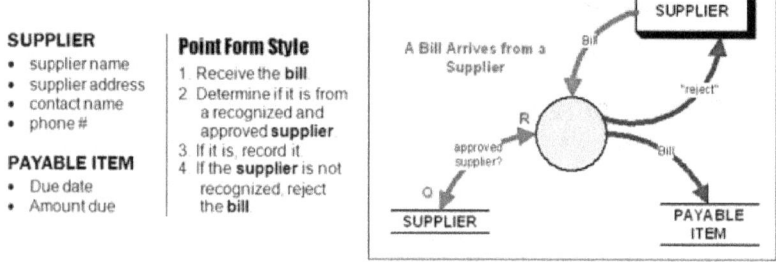

Fig. 98: Complete but Unnamed Business Process

But we haven't named the process yet, which is the last thing we do before we build out the **Business Rules Table**.

We didn't name the process earlier (as you wanted to do) because that would have created an unconscious bias to make the narrative fit the name of the process. We have found that one of the best ways of freeing our mind from any predetermined path, or bias, is to name the process last, after the narrative is written.

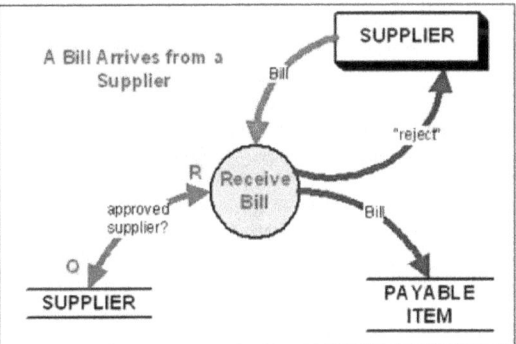

Point Form Style

1. Receive the **bill**.
2. Determine if it is from a recognized and approved **supplier**.
3. If it is, record it.
4. If the **supplier** is not recognized, reject the **bill**.

SUPPLIER
- supplier name
- supplier address
- contact name
- phone #

PAYABLE ITEM
- Due date
- Amount due

Fig. 99: Complete Business Process – with
Object descriptions, narrative and process name

Naming a process is a lot easier than it appears. The first word in the process label is <u>always a verb</u>. The next word or two is always the subject of the process. The subject usually includes a noun. For our example *business event* "**A Bill Arrives from a Supplier**" we have to ask ourselves, *What are we really doing here?* Since we are receiving a bill from a supplier we can name the process "Receive Bill". That gives us a strong verb and a subject.

Labels for processes must be strong and to the point, not abstractions. Abstractions that you want to stay away from include weak verbs such as "process" and "handle". For example, "Process Employee Pay" sounds like something we do to sausages. It's far better to say "Pay Employee". Another example of a weak label is, "Handle Payables", which sounds more like a juggling act than the more specific "Pay Supplier".

Examples of strong and pointy process labels include:

- Pay Supplier
- Open Account
- Ship Product
- Reserve Seat
- Receive Loan Application
- Receive Payment

Although we haven't completed the **Business Rules Table**, we have done the **Business Process Diagram**, so we can now check off this *business event* from our **Project Business Event List**.

Now that we have created a **Business Process Diagram** that describes part

Project Business Event List
■ ~~A Bill Arrives from a Supplier~~
■ **It is Time to Pay a Supplier**

Fig. 100: Project Business Event List

of the business requirement (i.e., the *essential* requirement, without defining how it will be implemented), we can proceed with the **Business Rules Table**, where we will define the remaining business requirements for this specific process.

Take the Objects that are in the "Receive Bill" **Business Process Diagram** and build up a **Business Rules Table** for those Objects, so we can ask a series of specific questions.

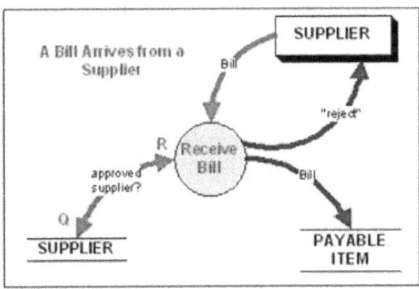

Fig. 101: Business Process Diagram –
"Receive Bill"

Build the table by placing the Objects SUPPLIER and PAYABLE ITEM found in the diagram (Fig. 101) into the rows and columns indicated in Fig. 102. Put a '1' in front of each of the Objects in the anchor position to the left. This will help you focus on a single occurrence of the anchor Object when you ask the questions that arise from this table.

	BRT	Supplier	Payable Item
1	Supplier	---	
1	Payable Item		---

Fig. 102: Basic Structure of a Business Rules
Table (BRT)

For the time being, blank out the intersection of like Objects, such as SUPPLIER+SUPPLIER and PAYABLE ITEM+-PAYABLE ITEM. We'll discuss those later.

After placing each of the Objects into the **Business Rules Table** that we found in the **Business Process Diagram**, we start with the first 'anchor' Object and ask the 'BRT Questions' of it. You can usually use the verb you assigned to the process ('receive') to structure the 'BRT Questions'.

PLACEHOLDER QUESTION: **"For a single, specific SUPPLIER how many PAYABLE ITEMs might we receive?"**

We don't wait for an answer to this first question. It is just a mental placeholder. We immediately go on with the three follow-on questions, soliciting a response from our subject-matter experts for each of them.

QUESTION # 1: **"Could we receive just one PAYABLE ITEM from the SUPPLIER?"**

This question isn't intended to exclude the two following questions, but your SMEs may be tempted to respond with an expanded answer such as, *"Yes, and we might get several bills from them…"* which already answers the next question. If the answer is **NO** we enter nothing in the cell joining the two Objects that make up the question. But if the answer is **YES**, we put a '1' in the **SUPPLIER+PAYABLE ITEM** intersection cell.

	BRT	Supplier	Payable Item
1	Supplier	---	1
1	Payable Item		---

Fig. 103: SUPPLIER and PAYABLE ITEM Relationship in "Receive Bill" Context

QUESTION # 2: **"Could we receive many PAYABLE ITEMs from the SUPPLIER?"**

This kind of closed-ended question tends to draw out specific responses. Again, if the answer is **NO** we enter nothing in the cell joining the two Objects that make up the question. But if the answer is **YES**, we put an **'N'** in the **SUPPLIER+PAYABLE ITEM** intersection cell (Fig. 104).

	BRT	Supplier	Payable Item
1	Supplier	---	1, N
1	Payable Item		---

Fig. 104: SUPPLIER and PAYABLE ITEM Relationship
in "Receive Bill" Context

QUESTION # 3: **"Might we never receive any PAYABLE ITEMs from the SUPPLIER at all?"**

Notice that this question does not ask, *"Could there be none…",* which is a completely different kind of question. What we're looking for here is, firstly, an exclusion from the possibility of any other answers than those given to the first two 'BRT Questions'. Secondly, we're looking for the inclusion of a possible exception as being part of normal business policy. In other words, this question serves the dual purpose of verifying answers already given, and a search for legitimate exceptions to those answers.

When there is a **YES** to this kind of question (i.e., *"We might **never** receive a **payable item** from a **supplier**…"*) we find that SMEs often like to discuss the exceptional situation at length, as if it was a newly discovered business policy.

On the other hand, if the answer is **NO** (i.e., *"We might **not ever** receive any **payable items** – therefore we will always receive one or more **payable items** from a **supplier**…"*) then we enter nothing in the cell joining the two Objects that make up the question. But if the answer is **YES**, we put a '**0**' in the **SUPPLIER+PAYABLE ITEM** intersection cell.

BRT		Supplier	Payable Item
1	Supplier	---	1, N, 0
1	Payable Item		---

Fig. 105: SUPPLIER and PAYABLE ITEM Relationship
in "Receive Bill" Context

Notice that we ask this third question from the perspective of all time; that is, the word "never" is intentionally chosen to mean just that – **never** – spanning all time. Time is an interesting element – it just keeps right on moving, no matter what we do. You certainly can substitute the words "not ever" if you wish.

When a client or subject matter expert answers "yes" to this third question, we must always follow up with a fourth question:

QUESTION # 4: **"Under what circumstances might that be true?"**

Let's partition this a bit more so we can understand it better.

All the suppliers that make up our **SUPPLIER** Object are "approved" suppliers. These are the only ones that are part of our list of suppliers. (It sort of makes sense that our list would not include the entire world of suppliers.)

In this example we have just asked the subject-matter expert, **"Might we never receive any PAYABLE ITEMs from the SUPPLIER at all?"** And the SME, quite reasonably replied, *"That's right, we might never receive a payable item from a supplier."*

The question, of course, is ... how does someone get to become an approved supplier, and yet we don't do any business with that supplier? To find out we have to ask the follow-up question **"Under what circumstances might that be true ...** *that we might never get a payable item from a supplier?***"** In this example, our client's answers could be several:

"They could have gone out of business before we ordered anything from them."

"We did order from the supplier, but they were never able to ship the product to us, so eventually we just stopped doing business with them."

Both of the above, and more, are possible answers in this circumstance. It is the analyst's responsibility, and challenge, to ferret out as much information as possible from the client or subject-matter experts.

So, what does it accomplish for us to uncover these "never" situations? Plain and simple, it goes directly to the issue of completeness of the business requirements. It enables us to find *business events* – situations or circumstances – that we may not have found previously. Remember that our definition of a *business event* is "... an essential business condition, a state, an external requirement, or <u>a circumstance</u> ..." and our fourth follow-on question is **"Under what <u>circumstances</u> might that be true?"** In other words, with this question, we're really looking for *business events*. And a complete business requirement means finding all the *business events* the target business area must deal with.

Let's look at each of the scenarios we have painted.

1. "They could have gone out of business before we ordered anything from them."

Based on this answer we must follow up with the subject-matter experts and ask if the *business event* **"The Supplier Goes Out of Business"** is something that could be within the scope of the project. For an Accounts Payable project, it seems reasonable that we would want to know if one of our suppliers went out of business. If our subject-matter expert says, *"Yes, we would like to know"* then add this new *business event* to the **Project Business Event List (Parking Lot)**.

Project Business Event List (Parking Lot)

- A Bill Arrives from a Supplier
- It is Time to Pay a Supplier
- The Supplier Goes Out of Business

Fig. 106: Business Event List "Parking Lot"
with Discovered Events

2. "We did order from the supplier, but they were never able to ship the product to us, so eventually we just stopped doing business with them."

From that answer we must follow up with the subject-matter expert and ask if the *business events* **"The Supplier is Unable to Fill the Product Order"** or **"Product Does Not Arrive from Supplier"** are circumstances we need to know about in our system. If so, are they within the scope of the project? If our subject-matter expert says, *"Yes, we need to know this"* then we add both new *business events* to our **Project Business Event List (Parking Lot)**, in Fig. 107. (We'll add both *business events* because they seem to be a little different.)

**Project Business Event List
(Parking Lot)**

- A Bill Arrives from a Supplier
- It is Time to Pay a Supplier
- The Supplier Goes Out of Business
- The Supplier is Unable to Fill the Product Order
- Product Does Not Arrive from Supplier

Fig. 107: Business Event List "Parking Lot"
with Discovered Events

There are other ways to find new *business events*, too. One of the best ways is simply by *listening* carefully to the client or SME. But listening for what? You will recall that we specified that suppliers must be "approved" before they can be on our list of suppliers. In this case we have to ask, *"How did the supplier get to be approved?"* Since it hasn't been covered yet, is there a *business event* such as "**Supplier Applies to Become an Approved Supplier**"? To find out we ask our SMEs. If their answer is, *"Yes, we receive applications from suppliers who want to become approved suppliers,"* then we add this to our list of new *business events* too, as in Fig. 108.

**Project Business Event List
(Parking Lot)**

- A Bill Arrives from a Supplier
- It is Time to Pay a Supplier
- The Supplier Goes Out of Business
- The Supplier is Unable to Fill the Product Order
- Product Does Not Arrive from Supplier
- Supplier Applies to Become an Approved Supplier

Fig. 108: Business Event List "Parking Lot"
with Discovered Events

As you can see, the process of going through the 'BRT Questions' produces a lot of information that goes directly to the heart of the project. The 'BRT Questions' not only help us find business rules (we'll get to the details of that in a moment), but they help us find hidden *business events* too, like the ones above.

Let's review.

We started with two original *business events* ("**A Bill Arrives from a Supplier**" and "**It is Time to Pay a Supplier**"), supported by two Objects (**SUPPLIER** and **PAYABLE ITEM**). We also attributed some data to the two Objects; and we found several new *business events* to add to our list. We also determined the ratio of occurrences (0, 1, N) between two Objects.

For the first *business event* that we worked on ("**A Bill Arrives from a Supplier**"), there now only remains the task of writing the business rules that come from the **Business Rules Table**, and to assign those rules to the right Objects.

	BRT	Supplier	Payable Item
1	Supplier	---	1, N, 0
1	Payable Item		---

Fig. 109: SUPPLIER and PAYABLE ITEM Relationship

For the first anchor Object – **SUPPLIER** – we know that we could receive one or several **PAYABLE ITEMs**, or we may never receive any at all, for which we have several examples. These rules (noted with the symbols **1,N,0**) must be documented as declarative statements in the correct context (i.e., with the proper verb) under the anchor Object **SUPPLIER**. In this example, the **PAYABLE**

ITEMs rules for **SUPPLIER** might read something like you see in Fig. 110 below.

SUPPLIER

Business Rules
- We can receive one or more **PAYABLE ITEM**s from a **SUPPLIER**

- We may never receive a **PAYABLE ITEM** from a **SUPPLIER** (e.g., may go out of business before we order a product; may not have been able to fill the only order from us).

Data Attributes
- supplier name
- supplier address
- contact name
- phone #

Fig. 110: SUPPLIER Business Rules

The next step is to ask the 'BRT Questions' of the second anchor Object, **PAYABLE ITEM**. Let's play it out.

PLACEHOLDER QUESTION: **"For a single, specific PAYABLE ITEM that we have received, how many SUPPLIERs might it come from?"**

Don't wait for an answer for this first question – it's your mental placeholder – just immediately go on with the three follow-on questions.

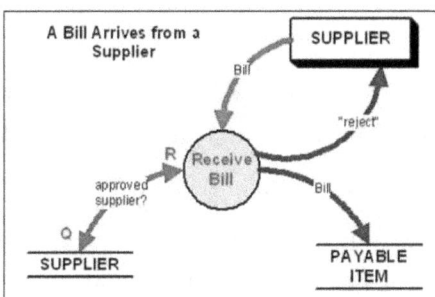

Fig. 111: Business Rules are in the Context of the Process for which the BRT was built

QUESTION # 1: **"Could the PAYABLE ITEM be from only one SUPPLIER?"**

In this example the answer from our subject matter experts is, *"Yes, of course, what did you think?* So, with a **YES** answer, we put a **'1'** in the **PAYABLE ITEM+SUPPLIER** intersection cell.

BRT		Supplier	Payable Item
1	Supplier	---	1, N, 0
1	Payable Item	1	---

Fig. 112: PAYABLE ITEM and SUPPLIER Relationship

QUESTION # 2: **"Could the PAYABLE ITEM be from several SUPPLIERs?"**

Our SME tells us the answer is **NO**, so we enter nothing in the cell joining the two Objects that make up the question.

BRT		Supplier	Payable Item
1	Supplier	---	1, N, 0
1	Payable Item	1	---

Fig. 113: PAYABLE ITEM and SUPPLIER Relationship

QUESTION # 3: **"Might the PAYABLE ITEM not be received from any SUPPLIER at all?"**

Once in a while this question addresses the intuitively obvious – such as this one. Of course, a payable item must come from an approved supplier, otherwise it can't be recognized as a payable item ... someone else's perhaps, but not ours. Even through the answer to the question seems self-evident, we still have to confirm with our subject-matter experts. The answer, of course, is *"No"* – a payable item must come from a supplier; therefore, we enter nothing new in the **PAYABLE ITEM+SUPPLIER** intersection cell.

BRT	Supplier	Payable Item
1 Supplier	---	1, N, 0
1 Payable Item	1	---

Fig. 114: PAYABLE ITEM and SUPPLIER Relationship

Sometimes, when there is a painfully obvious answer to a question you need to ask (such as verifying that a single, specific bill can only come from one supplier), it is easier to ask the client the 'BRT Question' differently than to try to solicit a double negative to mean *"yes"*. The question **"Might the PAYABLE ITEM not be received from any SUPPLIER at all?"** can cause, at the very least, a pained quizzical look on the face of the client or subject-matter expert. As they try to process this question, they are also wondering how you could ask such a question. What is probably going through their mind is the question, *"Say what?"*

A far better way of approaching this is to make a declarative statement with the answer, thus soliciting disagreement (which you probably won't get). For example, in this case, I would make the statement, **"And a PAYABLE ITEM can only come from one SUPPLIER, right?"** If they disagree, they will tell you. Otherwise, you'll get a fast nod of their collective heads and you can go on to the next questions or issues.

After you have asked the questions and got the answers, and entered them into the **Business Rules Table**, the new rules have to be written as declarative statements under the Object **PAYABLE ITEM**, which might read as in Fig. 115.

BRT		Supplier	Payable Item
1	Supplier	---	1, N, 0
1	Payable Item	1	---

PAYABLE ITEM

Business Rules
- A **PAYABLE ITEM** can be received from one **SUPPLIER** only.

Data Attributes
- Due date
- Amount due

Fig. 115: Business Rules for PAYABLE ITEM

The **Business Requirements Document** – the complete set of requirements documentation – is built incrementally. We record the requirements as we go through the analysis process and discover the business requirements with our clients and subject-matter experts. This incremental approach is possible because the requirements documentation doesn't have to be written serially or like a novel. In addition to being Object-based, it is focused on the individual **Business Process Diagrams**, and each component stands on its own. Therefore, the document is not produced serially, it is created in components based on the *business event*. For each *business event*, it includes the business process, Objects, data attributes, descriptive narrative, Business Rules Table, and context-specific business rules. This, in itself, speeds up the process significantly compared to old-school approaches.

To demonstrate this progression, let's look at the second *business event* on our list, "**It is Time to Pay a Supplier**".

**Project Business Event List
(Parking Lot)**

- A Bill Arrives from a Supplier
- It is Time to Pay a Supplier
- The Supplier Goes Out of Business
- The Supplier is Unable to Fill our Product Order
- Product Does Not Arrive from Supplier
- The Product Received from the Supplier is Defective
- Supplier Applies to Become an Approved Supplier

Fig. 116: Business Event List "Parking Lot"
with Discovered Events

Once again, the first question we ask is, *"How do I know that it is time to pay a supplier?"* The answer, of course, is *"We know because we have a due date."* You will recall earlier we attributed *due date* and *amount due* to the Object **PAYABLE ITEM**. The diagram and the accompanying data would, therefore, look like this, in Fig. 117 and 118.

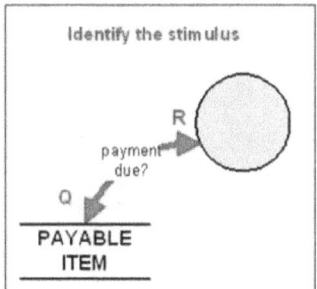

Identify the stimulus

R

payment due?

Q

PAYABLE ITEM

Fig. 117: Business Process
Queries "due date" to identify it
it is time to Pay Supplier

PAYABLE ITEM

Business Rules
- A **PAYABLE ITEM** can be received from one **SUPPLIER** only.

Data Attributes
- Due date
- Amount due

Fig. 118: PAYABLES ITEM
Data Attributes

This is also an example of where a stimulus that identifies a *business event* and initiates a process does not come from a Terminator, but instead comes from data that's part of an Object. This is the most common way of identifying if **"It is Time ..."** for something.

The second question is, *"What are we going to do about it?"* In this example our client told us that we pay the balance of the account after calculating any previous payments that were made to the supplier. Therefore, we must first determine if any previous payments to the supplier have been made.

To know if there were any previous payments we must have an Object called **PAYMENT**. Its data attributes would include *amount paid* (which includes previous payments), *date paid* and *method of payment*. There could be several previous payments.

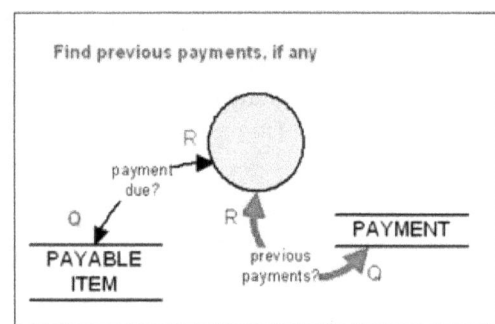

Fig. 119: Business Process Diagram and Object data – finding previous Payments

After we determined if there were any previous payments, we can calculate the remaining balance that's due.

We also need to identify the **SUPPLIER** we're going to send the payment to; and we can find that supplier by locating which one is linked to the **PAYABLE ITEM**.

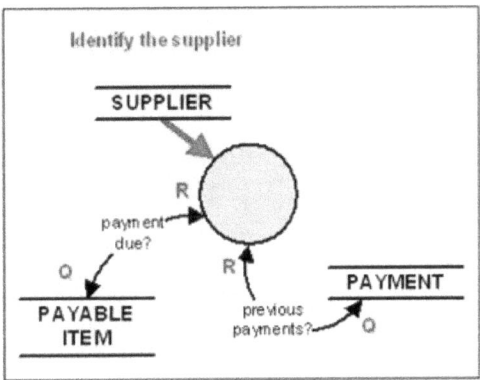

Fig. 120: Business Process identifies Supplier

And then we can send the payment to the supplier.

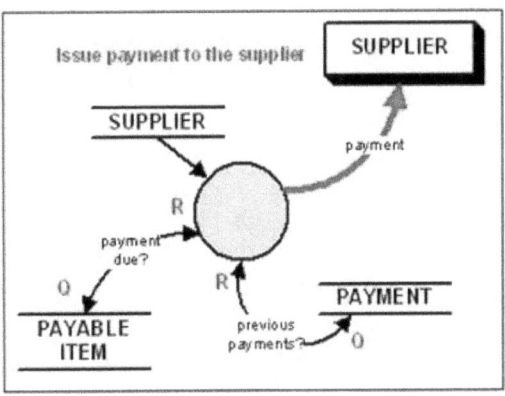

**Fig. 121: Business Process Issues
Payment to Supplier**

The last question to our subject matter expert is, *"What do we need to record or remember about this process?"* In this example we want to remember the payment sent to the supplier, including the method of payment and when it was made. We can draw this as illustrated in our diagram below (Fig. 122). The data attributes for the **PAYMENT** Object are also listed below.

PAYMENT

Data Attributes
- Amount paid
- Date paid
- Method of payment

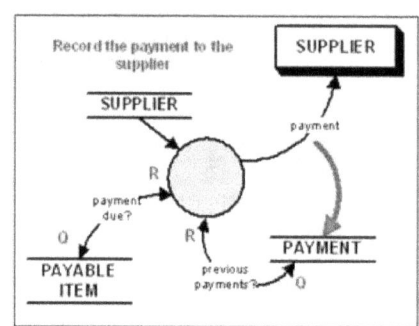

Fig. 122: Business Process Remembers Payment Issued

This now leaves us with a complete **Business Process Diagram** for the *business event* "**It is Time to Pay a Supplier**" (as shown in Fig. 123).

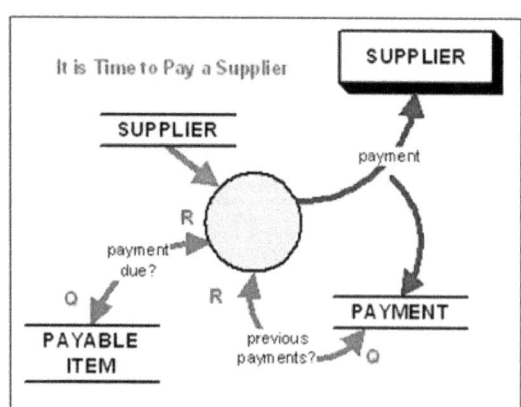

Fig. 123: Business Process almost done

But, once again, lots of things haven't been done yet. We still haven't named the process; nor have we written a descriptive narrative. We have only done a little bit of data attribution; and we haven't completed the **Business Rules Table** to define our business rules for the new Object, **PAYMENT**.

The very first question about this *business event* to our subject-matter experts was, *"How do I know that it is time to pay a supplier?"* This resulted in finding the stimulus (there was a *due date* for the **PAYABLE ITEM**), which eventually led to the full diagram.

As you draw the diagram for the process, your discussions with the subject-matter experts tend to bring out the remaining Objects and the data that make up the Objects. In this particular example, there are no more Objects or data needed to support the *business event* "**It is Time to Pay a Supplier**".

The next step is to write a descriptive narrative of the **Business Process Diagram**. The narrative has to be clear, concise, unambiguous, in plain business language – and brief.

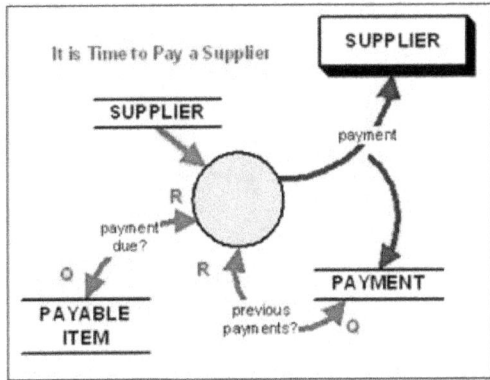

Fig. 124: Business Process needs a descriptive narrative

So far, we have left the bubble that represents the process unlabeled. The process name is only assigned after we have written the narrative necessary to support the diagram.

Our objective is to write a narrative that explains the **Business Process Diagram** in as much detail as necessary, but no more. Our narrative must be in plain language, without any technobabble. The end result must be a narrative that's easily understood by the client, subject-matter experts, and a technical team.

We determine the narrative needed by identifying the tasks associated with each data flow that comes into or goes out of the process. For our "**It is Time to Pay a Supplier**" *business event* example, it looks like the illustration in Fig. 125; although we don't draw those little nodes on our real documentation, we just write the narratives.

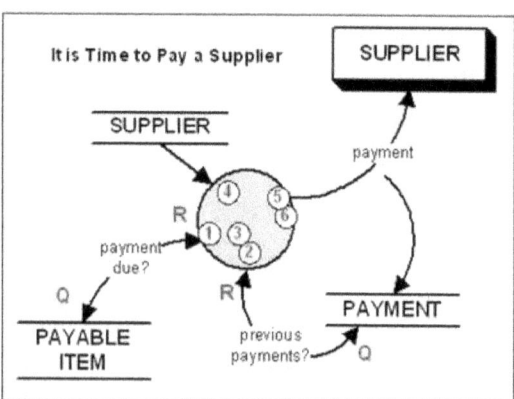

Fig. 125: Nodes identify tasks to be part of descriptive narrative

Each of these nodes must be referenced in some way in the narrative that you write. You can use at least two different styles when producing your narrative, the Structured Narrative Style, or the Point Form Style. You can also develop your own style, as long as your narrative text refers to each of the data flows entering or leaving the process. You may have to add additional text to describe the transformation of data, such as calculations or other formulas.

To write a narrative in this way is relatively easy and without pain. It enables you to quickly determine the tasks that make up a process without getting writer's block. Both types of narratives have been done for this example.

Point Form Style

1. Find bills (**PAYABLE ITEM**s) that are due to be paid.
2. Find previous **PAYMENT**s that have been made against individual bills (**PAYABLE ITEM**s), if any.
3. Determine the amount to be paid to a **SUPPLIER** (*amount due* minus previous *amount paid*).
4. Locate the **SUPPLIER** for the **PAYABLE ITEM**.
5. Pay the **SUPPLIER**.
6. Record the **PAYMENT**.

Structured Narrative Style

For each bill (**PAYABLE ITEM**) that is due for payment, determine the balance to be paid based on previous partial **PAYMENT**s against the bill. Pay the **SUPPLIER** and remember the **PAYMENT**.

Fig. 126: Two Styles of Process Narrative

We now have a complete diagram and narrative for the *business event* "**It is Time to Pay a Supplier**". We have also identified the Objects and data attributes we need to support the process.

But we haven't named the process yet, which is the last thing we do before we build out the **Business Rules Table** for this process.

You will recall that a *business event* name (such as "**It is Time to Pay a Supplier**") <u>never</u> starts with a verb. The name of the process that supports a *business event*, however, <u>always</u> starts with a verb.

So, what are we really doing in this process? We're sending a payment to a supplier; therefore, we can name the process "Pay Supplier". That gives us a strong verb and a subject.

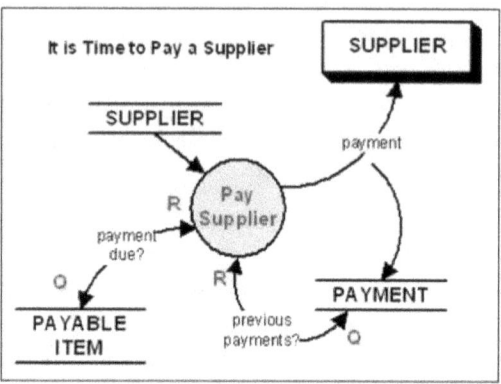

Fig. 127: A Named Business Process Diagram

Although we haven't completed the **Business Rules Table** for the new **PAYMENT** Object yet, we can now check off this *business event* from our **Project Business Event List (Parking Lot)**,

Project Business Event List (Parking Lot)

- A Bill Arrives from a Supplier
- It is Time to Pay a Supplier
- **The Supplier Goes Out of Business**
- **The Supplier is Unable to Fill our Product Order**
- **Product Does Not Arrive from Supplier**
- **Supplier Applies to Become an Approved Supplier**

Fig. 128: Making Progress against the
Business Event List "Parking Lot"

The **Business Rules Table** has to include all Objects that support a process. Although we did work through a BRT for the earlier process "Receive Bill" the context has now changed, so there will be different rules produced from the table. Therefore, all Objects that support the process "Pay Supplier" must be queried.

Take the Objects that are in the diagram for the "Pay Supplier" process and build up a **Business Rules Table** for those Objects.

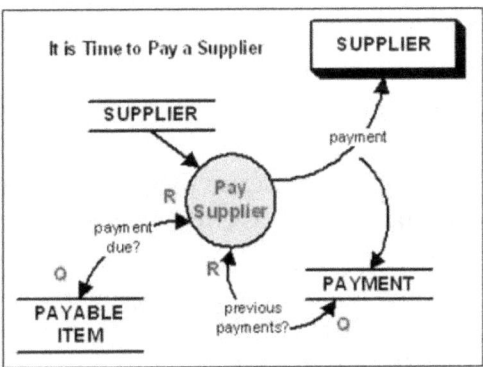

Fig. 129: Business Process Diagram – "Pay Supplier"

Build a table, just like the previous example, by placing the Objects (**SUPPLIER**, **PAYABLE ITEM** and **PAYMENT**) in the rows and columns indicated. Put a '**1**' in front of each of the Objects in the anchor position to the left. This will help you focus on a single occurrence of the anchor Object when you ask the questions that arise from this table.

	BRT	Supplier	Payable Item	Payment
1	Supplier	---		
1	Payable Item		---	
1	Payment			---

Fig. 130: Business Rules Table for "Pay Supplier"

For the time being, blank out the intersection of like Objects.

We can now start with the first 'anchor' Object and ask the 'BRT Questions'. You can usually use the verb you assigned to the business process (Fig. 129) to structure your 'BRT Questions'. If that verb doesn't work, then select another verb construct based on the concept behind the process. The idea is to ask the 'BRT Questions' based on the context of the process.

PLACEHOLDER QUESTION: **"For a single, specific SUPPLIER how many PAYABLE ITEMs might be due to be paid to them?"**

We don't wait for an answer to this first question. It is just a mental placeholder. We immediately go on with the three follow-on questions, soliciting a response from our subject-matter experts for each of them.

QUESTION # 1: **"Could there be just one PAYABLE ITEM due to be paid to a SUPPLIER?"**

Our SME answers, *"Yes, and there might be several bills to be paid to a supplier too…"* which already answers the next question. Since the answer is **YES**, we put a **'1'** in the **SUPPLIER+PAYABLE ITEM** intersection cell.

	BRT	Supplier	Payable Item	Payment
1	Supplier	---	1	
1	Payable Item		---	
1	Payment			---

Fig. 131: SUPPLIER and PAYABLE ITEM Relationship in Pay Supplier Context

QUESTION # 2: **"Could there be <u>many</u> PAYABLE ITEMs due to be paid to a SUPPLIER?"**

The answer is **YES**, so we put an **'N'** in the **SUPPLIER-PAYABLE ITEM** intersection cell.

	BRT	Supplier	Payable Item	Payment
1	Supplier	---	1, N	
1	Payable Item		---	
1	Payment			---

Fig. 132: SUPPLIER and PAYABLE ITEM Relationship in Pay Supplier Context

QUESTION # 3: **"Might we <u>never</u> have <u>any</u> PAYABLE ITEMs that are due to be paid to a SUPPLIER at all?"**

The answer is **YES**, so we put a **'0'** in the **SUPPLIER-PAYABLE ITEM** intersection cell.

	BRT	Supplier	Payable Item	Payment
1	Supplier	---	1, N, 0	
1	Payable Item		---	
1	Payment			---

Fig. 133: SUPPLIER and PAYABLE ITEM Relationship in Pay Supplier Context

When the answer is "yes" to this third question, we must always follow up with a fourth question:

QUESTION # 4: **"Under what circumstances might that be true?"**

"They could have gone out of business before we ordered anything from them."

"We did order from the supplier, but they were never able to ship the product to us, so eventually we just stopped doing business with them."

These are the same responses we got when we asked the SMEs about the **SUPPLIER+PAYABLE ITEM** relationship in the context of the **"Receive Bill"** process earlier. That being the case, we don't have to add any new *business events* to our list since they have all been added before.

	BRT	Supplier	Payable Item	Payment
1	**Supplier**	---	**1, N, 0**	
1	**Payable Item**		---	
1	**Payment**			---

Fig. 134: SUPPLIER and PAYABLE ITEM Relationship in Pay Supplier Context

Now we need to write the business rules for the new relationship (based on context of the "Pay Supplier" process, Fig. 135) between **SUPPLIER** and **PAYABLE ITEM**.

For the first anchor Object – **SUPPLIER** – we now know that we could issue a payment for one or

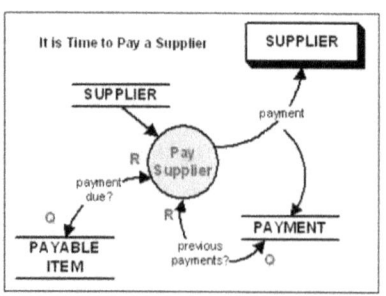

Fig. 135: Business Process Diagram for "Pay Supplier"

several **PAYABLE ITEM**s, or we may never pay any at all. These rules are documented as declarative statements under the anchor Object **SUPPLIER** (in the context of the "Pay Supplier" business process it supports). In this example, the **PAYABLE ITEM**s rules attributed to **SUPPLIER** might read something like those in Fig. 136.

SUPPLIER

Business Rules

- We can receive one or more **PAYABLE ITEM**s from a **SUPPLIER**.

- We may never receive a **PAYABLE ITEM** from a **SUPPLIER** (e.g., may go out of business before we order a product; may have sent us a defective product on their only order from us; may not have been able to fill the only order from us).

- ★ We can pay one or more **PAYABLE ITEM**s for a **SUPPLIER**.

- ★ We may never have a **PAYABLE ITEM** to pay for a **SUPPLIER** (e.g., may go out of business before we order a product; may not have been able to fill the only order from us).

Data Attributes

- supplier name
- supplier address
- contact name
- phone #

Fig. 136: SUPPLIER Business Rules

The next step is to ask the 'BRT Questions' of the next Object (**PAYMENT**) that intersect with the anchor Object **SUPPLIER**. Let's play this one out.

PLACEHOLDER QUESTION: **"For a single, specific SUPPLIER how many PAYMENTs might we issue (pay) to them?"**

We don't wait for an answer to this first question.

QUESTION # 1: **"Could we issue just one PAYMENT to a SUPPLIER?"**

Our SME answers, *"Yes, we might only ever make one payment to a supplier…"*. Put a **'1'** in the **SUPPLIER+PAYMENT** intersection cell.

BRT		Supplier	Payable Item	Payment
1	Supplier	---	1, N, 0	1
1	Payable Item		---	
1	Payment			---

Fig. 137: SUPPLIER and PAYMENT Relationship
in "Pay Supplier" Context

QUESTION # 2: **"Could we issue many PAYMENTs to a SUPPLIER?"**

The answer is **YES**, so we put an **'N'** in the **SUPPLIER+PAYMENT** intersection cell.

BRT		Supplier	Payable Item	Payment
1	Supplier	---	1, N, 0	1, N
1	Payable Item		---	
1	Payment			---

Fig. 138: SUPPLIER and PAYMENT Relationship in
"Pay Supplier" Context

QUESTION # 3: **"Might we never issue <u>any</u> PAYMENTs to a SUPPLIER at all?"**

The answer is **YES**, so we put a '**0**' in the **SUPPLIER+PAYMENT** intersection cell.

BRT	Supplier	Payable Item	Payment
1 Supplier	---	1, N, 0	1, N, 0
1 Payable Item		---	
1 Payment			---

Fig. 139: SUPPLIER and PAYMENT Relationship in
"Pay Supplier" Context

When the answer is "yes" to this question, we always follow up with a fourth question:

QUESTION # 4: **"Under what circumstances might that be true?"**

"While they were on our list of approved suppliers, we just never ordered anything from them."

This circumstance begs the question, *"Do we need to know about those suppliers who don't do business with us after a certain period of time?"* The answer from our subject-matter expert was *"No, we don't care,"* so we don't have to add any new *business events* to our list on the right.

Project Business Event List (Parking Lot)

- ~~A Bill Arrives from a Supplier~~
- ~~It is Time to Pay a Supplier~~
- The Supplier Goes Out of Business
- The Supplier is Unable to Fill our Product Order
- Product Does Not Arrive from Supplier
- Supplier Applies to Become an Approved Supplier

Fig. 140: Project Business Event List
"Parking Lot"

Now we need to write the business rules for the new relationship between **SUPPLIER** and **PAYMENT**. The **PAYMENT** rules attributed to **SUPPLIER** might read something like what you see in Fig. 141.

SUPPLIER

Business Rules

★ We can issue one or more
  PAYMENTs to a **SUPPLIER**.

★ We may never issue a **PAYMENT** to
  a **SUPPLIER** (e.g., we just didn't
  order anything from them).

Fig. 141: More SUPPLIER Business Rules

You go through exactly the same process for the other Objects that support the process "Pay Supplier", those Objects being **PAYABLE ITEM** and **PAYMENT**. When you're done, and you have all the answers to the questions, you will end up with the following entries in the **Business Rules Table**.

	BRT	Supplier	Payable Item	Payment
1	Supplier	---	1, N, 0	1, N, 0
1	Payable Item	1	---	1, N
1	Payment	1	1	---

Fig. 142: Business Rules Table (BRT) for "Pay Supplier" Process

The answers in the BRT spell out policy quite nicely:

* A specific **PAYABLE ITEM** can be from one **SUPPLIER** only. (Makes sense.)

* A specific **PAYABLE ITEM** can have one or several **PAYMENT**s made against it. (In effect, this says there can be partial payments.)

* A specific **PAYMENT** can only be issued to one **SUPPLIER**. (This, too, makes sense.)

* A specific **PAYMENT** can only be for one **PAYABLE ITEM**. (This is because, in our example, accounting is done on an open item basis rather than balance forward.)

All of these rules are attributed to their respective anchor Objects.

Earlier I asked you to blank out the intersection of like objects, such as the cells for **SUPPLIER+SUPPLIER**, **PAYABLE ITEM+PAYABLE ITEM** and **PAYMENT+PAYMENT**. That's because if we ask the same questions of these recursive relationships as we would of all the other Objects, we would find it very challenging.

	BRT	Supplier	Payable Item	Payment
1	Supplier	---	1, N, 0	1, N, 0
1	Payable Item	1	---	1, N
1	Payment	1	1	---

Fig. 143: The Remaining Questions to Ask in a Business Rules Table (BRT) for "Pay Supplier" Process

For example, for the "Pay Supplier" process, the series of 'BRT Questions' for PAYABLE ITEM would read as follows:

PLACEHOLDER QUESTION: **"For a single, specific PAYABLE ITEM how many other PAYABLE ITEMs might we pay for?"**

Say what? This doesn't seem to make a lot of sense.

QUESTION # 1: **"Could we pay for just one PAYABLE ITEM ... PAYABLE ITEM?"**

How do we even structure this question? There's clearly a problem here.

QUESTION # 2: **"Could we pay for many PAYABLE ITEMs .... PAYABLE ITEM?"**

Again, how do we even structure this question? This isn't working.

QUESTION # 3: **"Might we never pay any PAYABLE ITEMs ... PAYABLE ITEM at all?"**

What kind of sentence structure could we use to make this into a sensible question?

Of course, none of those questions work in this context – and they usually don't work when trying to ask questions about the relationship between like Objects. So how do we ask these important questions?

By changing how we ask.

If you are querying the intersection of like Objects – or even if the standard 'BRT Questions' just don't seem to work or don't make too much sense – then change how you ask the placeholder question to the following (in a "Pay Supplier" context):

SUPPLIER Substitute Placeholder Question: **"If I know about one SUPPLIER that we pay, under what circumstances would I ever want to find another, related SUPPLIER that we pay?**

PAYABLE ITEM Substitute Placeholder Question: **"If I know about one PAYABLE ITEM that we pay for, under what circumstances would I ever want to find another, related PAYABLE ITEM that we pay for?**

PAYMENT Substitute Placeholder Question: **"If I know about one PAYMENT that is issued to a supplier, under what circumstances would I ever want to find another, related PAYMENT to that supplier?**

The difference between this substitute placeholder Question and the regular one is that we do expect an answer from our subject-matter experts.

With this question, we are looking for a *circumstance* – which, as we know, is really a *business event*. The answers that our SMEs give us identify *business events* (circumstances) that may or may not already be on our **Project Business Event List (Parking Lot)**. Answers such as, *"We want to know about multiple payments to a supplier so we can determine how much business we're giving them"* will lead to a new *business event*, **"Company Wants to Know Historical Payments to a**

Supplier (for a Period)". If this *business event* – regardless of how it is stated – is already on the **Project Business Event List (Parking Lot)**, there's nothing to add to the list. If it's not, however, a new *business event* has been discovered and it has to be added to the list if it is determined to be in scope.

Project Business Event List
(Parking Lot)
- A Bill Arrives from a Supplier
- It is Time to Pay a Supplier
- The Supplier Goes Out of Business
- The Supplier is Unable to Fill our Product Order
- Product Does Not Arrive from Supplier
- Supplier Applies to Become an Approved Supplier
- Company Wants to Know Historical Payments to a Supplier (for a Period)

Fig. 144: Project Business Event List
"Parking Lot" with another Event Added

Once you have the answer to the substitute placeholder question, the regular three (or four) 'BRT Questions' still have to be asked of the subject Object.

Can the discovery of a *business event* lead to additional questions that, in turn, can find other *business events*? You bet. A good example is the one we just looked at.

The new *business event*, "**Company Wants to Know Historical Payments to a Supplier (for a Period)**" is essentially a report, regardless of the form it will finally take. Any time a report or a list is required, the question an analyst must ask is, *"If I know about the historical payments we made to a supplier, what does that tell us?"*

Earlier we looked at <u>Inclusion Questions</u> for Objects and data items. This same kind of question can be applied to potentially discover new *business events* from already identified *business events*.

The Inclusion Question (for Events)

"If we know about {<u>the EVENT</u>} what will it <u>enable</u> us to do that we could not do if we didn't know about it?"

The Exclusion Question (for Events)

"If we <u>do not know</u> about {<u>the EVENT</u>} what will it *<u>prevent</u>* us from doing that we must be able to do?"

What kind of answers might you get?

INCLUSION: **"If we know about** {<u>the historical</u> <u>payments to a supplier (for a period)</u>} **what will it <u>enable</u> us to do that we could not do if we didn't know about it?"**

Answer: *"It enables us to do comparative research of how much business we're doing with certain suppliers so we can negotiate better financial terms with some of them."*

EXCLUSION: **"If we do not know about** {<u>the</u> <u>historical payments to a supplier (for a period)</u>} **what will it <u>prevent</u> us from doing that we must be able to do?"**

Same answer, different perspective: *"It would prevent us from knowing how much business we're doing with certain suppliers, which would in turn prevent us from negotiating better financial terms with some of them."*

Both answers suggest another *business event* not previously discovered, "**It is Time to Negotiate Better Financial Terms with a Supplier**", which must be added to our list.

When an identified *business event* is essentially a report or a list of some kind – regardless of how it will actually be designed and implemented – you must take it one more step and ask *"What does that tell us?"* or *"What does it prevent us from doing if we don't have it?"*

Finding reports or lists to be produced is one of the easier things to do. Clients and SMEs will always have a long list of reports and lists they want. For a business analyst to simply accept a requirement for a list or report is not analysis, it's just regurgitation of what the subject matter-expert thinks

Project Business Event List (Parking Lot)
• ~~A Bill Arrives from a Supplier~~
• ~~It is Time to Pay a Supplier~~
• **The Supplier Goes Out of Business**
• **The Supplier is Unable to Fill our Product Order**
• **Product Does Not Arrive from Supplier**
• **Supplier Applies to Become an Approved Supplier**
• **Company Wants to Know Historical Payments to a Supplier (for a Period)**
• **It is Time to Negotiate Better Financial Terms with a Supplier**

Fig. 145: Project Business Event List "Parking Lot" with another Event Added

should be done. But please note that the SME is not a business analyst. You are. And you are the one that has to do the analysis to find out what the real requirements are, rather than the surface requirements. And a report or list is a surface requirement because people <u>*do something*</u> with reports, usually to uncover other information that's not directly on the report. While this isn't always the case, it often is.

Finally, from our two starting *business events* ("**A Bill Arrives from a Supplier**" and "**It is Time to Pay a Supplier**") we managed to get all of this:

1. Two **Business Process Diagrams** (*Receive Bill* and *Pay Supplier*).
2. A descriptive narrative for each of the two business processes.
3. Discovery of three Objects (**PAYABLE ITEM, SUPPLIER** and **PAYMENT**).
4. The necessary data attributes for each of the three Objects.
5. Business rules for each of the three Objects.
6. A list of six (6) additional *business events* that had not been found originally.

As an added benefit, we also got a prescription for database design (the required data accesses) based on the business requirements. For database designers, the notation (0,1,N) in the **Business Rules Table** translates directly into the accesses required in a Conceptual Data Model, while the Objects with data attributes provides the composition of the data model.

4.3 The Non-Serial Incremental Approach

Business requirements for any project are developed incrementally, but it certainly should never be done serially. Using the approach in this book, you can uncover the processes, data and business rules for any *business event* at any time, in any sequence. Each can stand on its own during discovery sessions. Although many Objects are shared by different business processes, there isn't any dependency by one process on another; therefore, the sequence with which you analyze the different *business events* is unimportant. The only thing that matters is your comfort level with the sequence in which you work.

Most organizations with business systems are mature, integrated and complex; therefore, there isn't just one 'beginning' for the analyst on a project. There could be many 'beginnings', depending on the number of business areas involved and on their perspectives. Most projects in mature organizations involve several business areas; therefore, there are often as many perspectives on where things begin and end, as there are business areas represented.

This non-serial approach to analysis is also possible because the **Business Requirements Document** doesn't have to be written sequentially either. The document that's produced to define the business requirements, just like the business, should not be a serial description of business processes, like the old manufacturing or paper flow systems from the past. In today's world, that would be difficult to produce, although I see that many people still try. The document you produce should be organized by *business event* (business condition), which is then a whole lot easier to read and understand.

Part 5.
Conclusion

One of the biggest challenges for any analyst is the awkard issue of how to get a project started as quickly as possible. An analyst needs to be visible and productive just about right away because, well, clients think of them as people who can walk on water while so many others pass water. But, as we all know, analysts come in to an organization, have little background on what makes it tick or who has the knowledge, and are expected to become visibly productive just about right away. Well, here's a plan that has always worked for me.

5.1 The 5-Point Project Plan

Any plan to uncover and specify business system requirements must be <u>specific</u> and <u>measurable</u>, not just another item on the list to be checked off. A plan must clearly identify what's to be done, by whom, and when. It must specify accurately the time and schedule involved. And it must be measurable – or it's just more of the **S**ame **O**ld **S**tuff made up of guesswork, magic numbers and unicorns.

1. **Initiate & Plan.** Working with your client …

    *   Identify the "co-pilot(s)" for the project. Whenever possible, you should have at least one. As the senior analyst, you are the Pilot.

    *   Document project rationale, mandate, perceived scope, identified risks, expectations, and project budget.

- Stakeholders and subject-matter experts should be identified and their involvement clearly defined.

- Describe the discovery session schedule. The initial entry will be the *Project Scope Blitz* (see below), while the schedule for the detailed discovery sessions will be filled in later.

- Create a detailed list and definition of the deliverables and artifacts expected from the project business requirements analysis. This will be integrated into the overall Project Plan, which – if it entails staggered or phased delivery – must also include phased business analysis. This, too, is dependent on the outcome of the *Project Scope Blitz* (see below).

- Define the metrics or Key Performance Indicators required to measure business analysis "success" for the project. Your success indicators will include, but are not limited to, a complete **Business Process Diagram** and all accompanying documentation for each *business event* identified; and documented business rules from each entry in the **Business Rules Table**.

- Define the acceptance and "sign off" process for the business requirements.

Outcome: <u>Business Analysis Plan</u>.

2. **Conduct Project Scope Blitz.** Even if your client believes they have the scope all figured out, you will still conduct a *Project Scope Blitz*.

Stakeholders and SMEs must participate in a ½-day or 1-day *Project Scope Blitz*. This highly interactive discovery session identifies clearly the conditions and circumstances the business must deal with (for your project), at a workable *business event* level, as well as the business areas and departments involved at each stage of business analysis. This enables you to schedule detailed discovery sessions. It also sets the tone for the project, right up front, and establishes your credibility as a servant leader and business analyst.

Outcome: <u>Project Business Event List</u>.

3. **Plan Detailed Discovery Sessions.** Based on the *Project Business Event List*, create a schedule for each detailed discovery session and the SMEs that are required to participate. Also, define the exact amount of time required to complete the project's business requirements analysis. (The metric we use is: 4 hours per *business event*, consisting of a 1-hour discovery session with clients and 3 hours to complete the analysis and documentation.)

The resulting schedule is highly dynamic, based on your SMEs' availability and other priorities by the client. However, deadlines can be set at this time.

Outcome: <u>Project Discovery Schedule</u>.

4. **Conduct Detailed Discovery Sessions.** Based on the *Project Discovery Schedule*, invite the identified subject-matter experts and conduct interactive one-hour discovery sessions for each *business event* to complete the business requirements for the project. Complete the remaining documentation for each *business event*.

Outcome: <u>Business Requirements Document</u>.

5. Coordinate Business Analysis Completion.
Depending on your mandate, you – as the business
analyst and "Pilot" for the project – will coordinate
completion of the business analysis part of the
project. The project may be phased or staged, which
usually means you will "Pilot" each stage of
business analysis. It will almost certainly extend
into the solution design or software acquisition
stage. If this is the case, it would be most productive
if you were part of the team guiding the technology
team through the business requirements.

Lessons learned from all the discovery sessions are
also integrated and documented now.

Outcome: <u>Business Analysis Project Review</u>.

5.2 What Really is an 'Agile' Project?

An "agile" project or agile environment is really a frame
of mind, rather than a process. It's a paradigm or mental
model of how we can approach our work. It's certainly
not a methodology. An agile environment simply means
– allow project teams to adapt working practices
according to the needs of the individual project.

The emphasis must be on delivering business value
early, and then to continually improve it. "Delivering
business value early" does not just refer to
implementing software; it means to deliver value in how
you interact with your business partners, clients and
subject-matter experts ... and how you are seen to do so.

It also means <u>don't do anything you don't have to do</u>
and try to think outside the box to <u>minimize doing things
in a certain way just because they have always been</u>

done that way. But, to accomplish this you also have to recognize that (a) you are doing something that you may not need to do; and (b) what you're doing is only being done that way because it has always been done that way. In other words, you have to be aware of the conflict, which is easier said than done. If you're not an expert in the conventional approach, then how would you know if a different approach is better? What's your benchmark? What do you compare to? And, to make it even more challenging, Thomas Kuhn, in his controversial book *"The Structure of Scientific Revolutions"* used the term "paradigm shift". He argued that rival paradigms are incommensurable – that is, it is not possible to understand one paradigm through the conceptual framework and terminology of another rival paradigm. I would certainly agree with that.

So, your opinion that something that's called for should not be done better have a sound foundation.

'Agile' doesn't mean doing something differently just because you can do it differently. 'Agile' doesn't mean doing less of the project, just to beat the clock. 'Agile' means knowing which best practices really are "best" rather than conventional. There are lots of so-called best practices heralded by maintainers of the *status quo*. Bear in mind that "best practices" have usually been around a long time for them to be accepted as best practices by the community. Some of these "best practices" have passed their *best before* dates.

Also, 'agile' does not mean chaos on the project team. It means finding the straightest road to the planned destination, and then taking that road even when others think you should take the most circuitous and bureaucratic route possible.

'Agile' also means learning new methods and techniques, not blindly sticking with methods that haven't changed in years, and without any indication things are getting better. It also means to not avoid doing what's required (some of the administrative things) just because it seems faster that way. Times change; methods change.

Above all, if you want to foster an agile environment, involve your clients and subject-matter experts in requirements discovery, and involve them a lot.

Your business requirements documentation should be in business language, and as brief as possible. And a client should not be expected to learn the technology you're using.

Recognize that you serve your client – whether that client is part of an internal group or a customer outside your organization – and you need their help and active participation to understand their requirements.

Recognize that requirements will change as your client understands better the information they want and can have. It's not a bad thing to "change your mind" when you have more information. As the famous British economist John Maynard Keynes once said, *"When the facts change, I change my opinion. What do you do?"* The issue is how to deal with those changes, since history tells us that change is good. This is what learning is all about, so when a client or subject-matter expert changes their mind, don't think *"not on my project."* This is actually a move in the right direction.

I believe very strongly that requirements analysis should be focused on individual *business events*, and their supporting processes, rather than trying to write a novel about how a system should work.

By focusing on the individual *business event* and its supporting processes and data, you can respond very quickly to any change that is needed. It minimizes the complexity of changing page after page in a serial novel. In event-based analysis, as described in this book, there is no redundancy; therefore, there is no domino effect in the documentation. It allows the business analyst to respond rapidly, while it gives the client or subject-matter expert the confidence to contribute without fear of criticism of "constantly changing their mind". Also, the direct 'BRT Questions' keep them highly focused, and they won't wander all over the scope of the requirements.

In my opinion, "agile" means being fast and responsive, but without chaos and risk.

An event-based approach to business requirements analysis is extremely fast, and without risk. The alternative – conventional system analysis that usually takes a long time – often leads to abbreviated requirements analysis (*"we finished when we ran out of time"*), which in turn leads to incomplete work down the line, and perhaps costly rework later on.

Some people refer to this event-based analysis approach as a "methodology". Well, so be it. I prefer to call it a paradigm – a constructive framework – which focuses on the following:

- *what* is to be observed and scrutinized
- the kind of *questions* that are supposed to be asked and probed for answers in relation to the subject
- *how* the questions are to be structured

- *how* the results of the investigations should be interpreted

In the end, quality of work is always directly related to education, experience, professional development, and the quality of the methods used and thinking applied.

So, always use good methods and clarity of thinking. Use modern methods. Practice using good methods and thinking.

You will get very good at this by – yes, you guessed it – by practice. Just do it. Make mistakes. It's the only way we know of to become expert at anything.

Trond Frantzen
trond.frantzen@powerstartgroup.com

Glossary

Agile Environment: An "agile" business analysis environment simply means, try to think outside the box to <u>minimize doing things in a certain way just because they have always been done that way</u>. "Agile" does not mean chaos on the project team. It means finding the straightest road to your destination, and then taking that road even when others think you should take the most circuitous and bureaucratic route possible.

Anchor Object: An Object is an 'anchor' or 'cardinal' Object when it is used in the **Business Rules Table** to describe its relationship with other Objects and to define its business policies. It is the stable 'anchor' that is the subject of any question that is asked about its relationship with other participating Objects. This approach stipulates that every Object in a relationship is equally important (which certainly eliminates the high subjectivity of figuring out which one is *most important,* which is required by some methodologies) and therefore

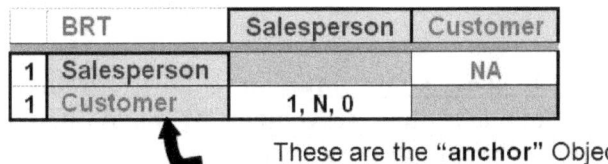

BRT		Salesperson	Customer
1	Salesperson		NA
1	Customer	1, N, 0	

These are the **"anchor"** Objects

must be queried about its relationship with other Objects in a relationship. Since it takes two to make a relationship, each of the two Objects (from their own perspective) are the most important. Accordingly, every Object is the 'anchor' to a question. See also **'Object'.**

Associative Object: An associative Object is an Object identified and created to remember essential information required in response to the occurrence of a *business event*. While it has all the attributes of any other kind of Object, it is also (a) dependent on some of the other Objects that participate in the same relationship; and (b) is created from the data that arises out of the process which supports the underlying relationship, since this new data cannot be found (by way of a *foreign key*) in any of the other Objects that participate in the same relationship. See also **'Object'**.

BRD: See **'Business Requirements Document'**.

BRT: See **'Business Rules Table'**.

Business Event: A *business event* is an essential business circumstance, condition, situation, state or external requirement that exists which the target business area must respond to or deal with in order to carry on operations to successfully support its key business objectives, goals, mission, direction and vision.

Business Process Diagram: This is an illustration of retrieval of data, the movement of data, and the recording of required data in a business process. A single Business Process Diagram can support one or more *business events*. Each diagram must also have a narrative written in plain language to describe it. Objects that appear in a diagram must also be defined, with their data attributes, as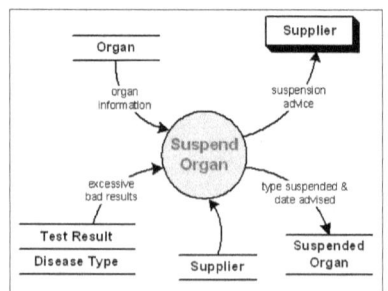

well as the business rules that govern the behavior and existence of the Objects.

Business Requirements Document: The Business Requirements Document is all the documentation needed to represent all the business needs for a particular business area, project or system. It consists of diagrams showing all the required business processes, including descriptive narratives, Object definitions, data items that belong to Objects, and the business rules that govern the behavior and existence of the Objects. This document should be as free of technology bias as possible; i.e., it should document what is needed but not how it will be implemented.

Business Rule: These are the rules that govern the behavior and existence of Objects that support the business processes. Business rules are documented as simple declaratives under each Object (to which the rule is attributed) in plain language.

SUPPLIER

Business Rules
- We can receive one or more **PAYABLE ITEM**s from a **SUPPLIER**.
- We may never receive a **PAYABLE ITEM** from a **SUPPLIER** (e.g., may go out of business before we order a product; may not have been able to fill the only order from us).

Business Rules Table: This table is a unique tool that enables the discovery of the rules that govern the behavior and existence of Objects that support the

BRT	Salesperson	Customer	Outlet	Product	Payment
1 Salesperson		N,0	1,N	N,0	N,0
1 Customer	1,N,0		1,N	1,N,0	1,N,0
1 Outlet	N	N		N	N
1 Product	1,N,0	1,N,0	1,N		1,N,0
1 Payment	1,N	1	1	1,N	

business requirements. It ensures the completeness of the business requirements by using a specific syntax to determine the questions to be asked to uncover the rules (the 'BRT Questions'). It also identifies the 'ratio of occurrences' between Objects, therefore creating a prescription for eventual database design based on the business requirements.

Cardinality: This is the "ratio of occurrences" between pairs of Objects; i.e., 0, 1 and N, or any combination of these. See also **'Business Rules Table'**.

Characteristic Object: When two or more *related and inseparable* data items are discovered, each having multiple values for a single instance of an Object, this data group is separated from the original Object in which it was present, to form a new and distinct Object. For example, if a SUPPLIER Object has several locations, then data attributes like *supplier address* and *supplier city* will be part of a multi-valued (repeating) group. This multi-valued group of data items is separated from the originating or parent Object, and named SUPPLIER LOCATION, and is "characteristic" of the original Object.

Client: A client is one of the key stakeholders on a project. The client can also be one of the project's subject-matter experts.

Data Attribute: A data attribute is an element of data belonging to an Object. A data attribute is described by a name and description, and eventually represented by a set of standard values, including sounds and images. Data attributes are required to define what must be remembered or known about each Object. See also **'Object'**.

PRODUCT
Data Attributes
• product description
• product photos & views (mv)
• examples of use (mv)
• product demonstrations (mv)
• product sounds (mv)
• reorder point
• product selling price
• volume discount available
• delivery lead time
• payment options (mv)
• product availability

Data Flow: A data flow represents the directional flow of information between a process and an Object or a Terminator.

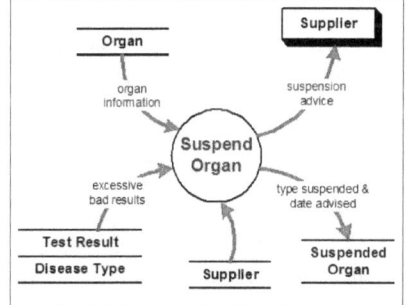

Discovery Session: See **'Requirements Discovery Session'**.

Exclusion Question (for Data): A question that identifies the consequences of excluding a data item by finding the *business event* the data item would otherwise support. See also **'Inclusion Question (for Data)'**.

Exclusion Question (for Objects): A question that identifies the consequences of excluding an Object by finding the *business event* the Object would otherwise support. See also **'Inclusion Question (for Objects)'**.

Exclusion Question (for Events): A question that identifies the consequences of excluding a *business event*. See also **'Inclusion Question (for Events)'**.

Exclusion Question (for Reports): A question that identifies the consequences of excluding a Report by finding the *business event* the Report would otherwise support. See also **'Inclusion Question (for Reports)'**.

Foreign Key: A foreign key is an Object's unique identifier contained within another Object. The foreign key provides the ability to find information from other related Objects to support the information needs of a specified business process. A foreign key is essentially an index or a pointer that 'joins' one Object to other related Objects. The 'joining' of Objects in this manner eliminates the need for redundant data repetition. A foreign key can be single-valued (i.e., point to <u>one</u> occurrence of another object); or it can be multi-valued (i.e., point to <u>several</u> instances of another Object). The ratio of occurrences (cardinality) between Objects is determined from the **Business Rules Table**.

CABLE ACCOUNT
Unique Identified
Cable Account-ID
Foreign Keys
Customer-ID (mv)
Rental-ID (mv)
Solution-ID (mv)
Promotion-ID (mv)

Inclusion Question (for Data): A question that identifies the necessity to include a data item by finding the *business event* the data item supports. See also **'Exclusion Question (for Data)'**.

Inclusion Question (for Objects): A question that identifies the necessity to include an Object by finding the *business event* the Object supports. See also **'Exclusion Question (for Objects)'**.

Inclusion Question (for Events): A question that identifies the necessity to include a *business event* by finding the consequences of including the *business event* (and therefore another *business event*). See also **'Exclusion Question (for Events)'**.

Inclusion Question (for Reports): A question that identifies the necessity to include a Report by finding the *business event* the Report supports. See also **'Exclusion Question (for Reports)'.**

Multi-valued (Repeating) Group: See **'Characteristic Object'.**

Normalization: "Normalization" is a commonly accepted method of eliminating data redundancies. The science underlying normalization theory is quite complex and normally requires considerable study. However, only researchers and teachers need this degree of familiarity with normalization theory and all its abstractions. Business analysts need to know how to do it so good Objects can be defined to support business processes – 'good' meaning Objects that are focused, and not a mixed bag of all kinds of data about all kinds of stuff. Knowing the details of the theory does not enhance our ability to deliver a business requirement with "fully normalized" data to support it. Scores of books have been written about this subject, so you can learn as much about the underlying theory as you want by searching on the Internet or buying a few good technical books. But to get a "normalized" data set for your project simply means following the **5 Rules of Business Data**. These Rules, when followed, will deliver a view of the data that is sufficiently "normalized" with redundancies minimized.

It should be noted that the conventional view is that normalization is "done" after all the needed data has been gathered and attributed to Objects, in a step-wise progression through different levels of normalization. While this does work, it also takes a very long time to do, and is very frustrating to people who want to get on with the work. The conventional approach is not an agile approach.

Using the methods in this book, normalization is done immediately when specific data is discovered. The data attribution rules are applied <u>during the process of data discovery</u>, not afterwards. Accordingly, it's done right away as a natural and inherent part of business system analysis. See also **'Denormalization'.**

Object: Objects that appear in Business Process Diagrams are the exact same Objects as defined in an Object-Relationship Diagram. Objects that are present in a process diagram were often called "data stores" in their earlier incarnation.

See also **'Business Process Diagram'.**

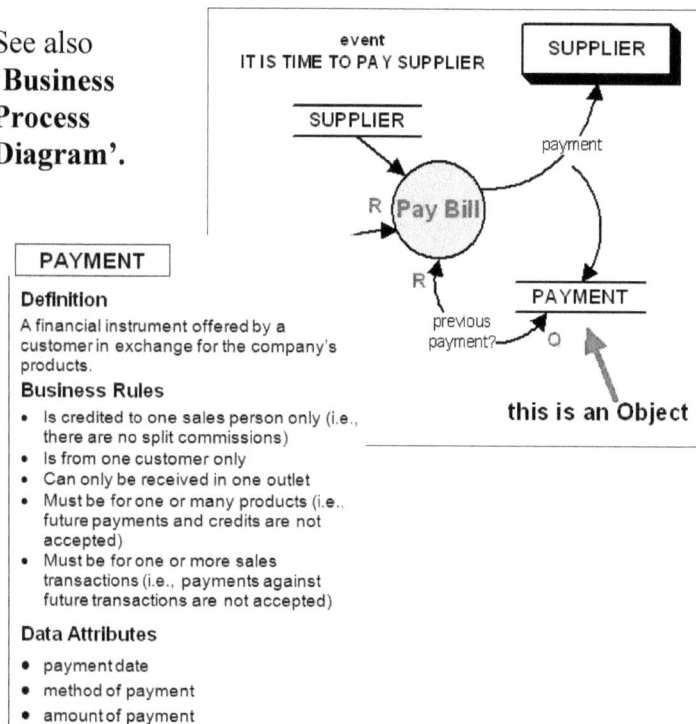

PAYMENT

Definition

A financial instrument offered by a customer in exchange for the company's products.

Business Rules

- Is credited to one sales person only (i.e., there are no split commissions)
- Is from one customer only
- Can only be received in one outlet
- Must be for one or many products (i.e., future payments and credits are not accepted)
- Must be for one or more sales transactions (i.e., payments against future transactions are not accepted)

Data Attributes

- payment date
- method of payment
- amount of payment
- type of card
- card expiry date

Process Narrative: A Business Process Diagram must always have a narrative written in plain language to describe it. The narrative can be written in several styles, the most common being 'Point Form Style' and the 'Structured Narrative Style'.

Point Form Style

For each request for a product from the customer:

- Find out if the customer exists in our system.
- Find the product sold.
- If it is available, give it to the customer with the price.
- Accept the payment from the customer.
- Remember the payment.
- Remember the salesperson who served the customer, and in which outlet.
- Reduce inventory by the quantity of product sold.
- If it is a new customer, get the customer information from the customer.
- Remember the new customer information.

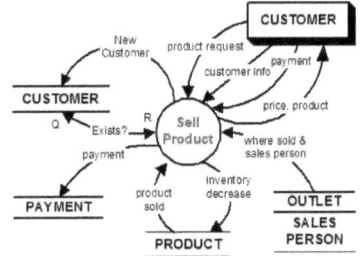

Structured Narrative Style

For each request for a product from the customer, find the product. If it is available give it to the customer with the cost. Accept the payment from the customer. Remember the payment and the sales transaction, including the sales person who served the customer, and in which outlet. Reduce inventory by the quantity of the product sold. If it is a new customer, remember the customer.

Ratio of Occurrences: See **'Cardinality'.**

Requirements Discovery Session: An interactive meeting of project clients and subject-matter experts, led by an expert "Pilot" and possibly supported by an expert "co-pilot", with the purpose of discovering business requirements.

SME: See also **'Subject-Matter Expert'.**

Subject-Matter Expert: An individual who may or may not be the client. Subject-matter experts are individuals who have all the required knowledge about the business areas and information that's involved in the targeted processes. A subject-matter expert should never be a surrogate client who does not work hands-on in the business area for which they are expert.

Subtype Object: A "subtype Object" (a.k.a. 'subclass') is a type of Object which has only those data attributes that are specific to a particular view of the Object (i.e., the subtype). Data attributed to one subtype Object cannot be attributed to any other Object. Data which is common to more than one subtype is attributed to the Object associated with the subtype, which is called a supertype Object. Each subtype Object must be associated with only one supertype Object. See also **'Supertype Object'** and **'Object'**.

Supertype Object: A "supertype Object" (a.k.a. 'superclass') is an Object that has several different views of the information it represents, with each distinct view known as a subtype Object. Each subtype of a supertype Object has unique and distinct data attributes. Supertype Objects contain only the data attributes that are common to all its subtypes. See also **'Subtype Object'** and **'Object'**.

Terminator: A Terminator is an external entity over which the business process it communicates with has no control. The Terminator can be outside the organization, or inside, but it is always external to the process that communicates with it. It acts as a source of input information, or a destination of information from the business process, but the processes and data inside a terminator are outside the scope of the target system. Many (but

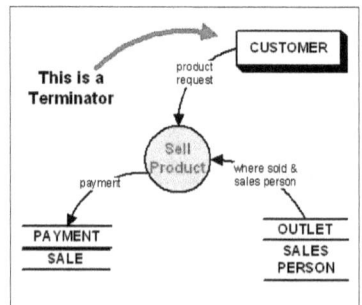

not all) terminators are also Objects, since we usually have to remember something about them.

Unique Identifier: A primary identifier or *key* is a unique identifier of a specific instance of an Object. The unique identifier should never contain data to be used in a process. It is simply a locator address. See also **'Object'.**